The Power of
Openness and Trust

THE
POWER
OF
OPENNESS
AND TRUST

HOW TO INCREASE THE IMPACT OF YOUR MANAGEMENT TEAM

LARS J CLEMEDSON

MCP
BOOKS

MCP Books
2301 Lucien Way #415
Maitland, FL 32751
407.339.4217
www.millcitypress.net

Printed in the United States of America

ISBN-13: 978-1-54562-642-9

CONTENTS

Why this framework?
Role patterns and behavioral expectations
Complexity or Simplification
The Importance of Feedback
Exposure and Defensiveness

History of Company X
The Situation at the Outset
  Inefficient decision-making
  Decisions are not implemented to full effect . . . .
  *Management lacks credibility as a model for the rest of
  the company*
  *The management team did not discuss any of
  these issues*
Positive Aspects of Company X
Summary of the management team's situation
Discrepancy between words and actions
  Lack of attention
  Benefits of not seeing
The aim for the developmental process

  He who sees the problem becomes the problem
  Apparent matter-of-factness
Linear versus non-linear logic

PREFACE

"Today we need just one management team meeting to solve problems that took us five meetings a year ago." So said Erling Ihle, CEO of a Scandinavian trading company, during his interview with a European business magazine.[1] When the reporter asked, "How come?" Ihle replied, "Today we just tell it like it is."

Ihle and his direct reports were the first managers with whom I worked using the approach described in this book, *Openness and Trust: How to Increase the Impact of Your Management Team.* Finally, after almost a decade of applying the methods which were—and still are—prevalent in the leadership training industry, I saw profound and sustainable change as a direct result of my work with Ihle's company. Unsolved issues and conflicts that had cost millions for many years were suddenly being solved in days or hours; commitment, motivation, and mutual accountability increased, boosting performance beyond expectation; absences due to

---

[1] *Svenska Dagbladet,* 24 October 1993.

illness or stress diminished significantly; and the bottom line result, in comparison with the company's competitors, sky-rocketed. It was also the first, but far from the last time my team would get the feedback that was the strongest evidence of real change: The wife of a middle-aged manager sent us a message thanking us for giving her back the vital and sensitive man she had married 25 years earlier.

In 2015, American companies spent $16 billion on leadership training; roughly $200-300 billion have been spent over the last 25 years. Despite these numbers, 65% of American employees reported to Forbes, in 2012, that they would rather "get rid" of their boss than get a raise—hardly an acceptable outcome of a multi-billion-dollar investment. Evaluations of leadership development programs generally show an infinitesimally small long-term effect on leader behavior, and, if measured at all, almost none on bottom line results. These facts scream of a leadership training industry that is in urgent need of new ways to improve leadership and management team performance. *Openness and Trust* makes a solid, proven contribution to that need.

One reason for the poor outcome of many leadership development programs is that both managers and leadership trainers have a predilection for simple cause–effect models that don't take the complexity of human interaction into consideration. The same tendency can be seen in other fields where people tries to exert influence on others. To give an example: when I studied psychology many years ago, I had the opportunity to observe the interaction between a social worker and her client, a man in his fifties, apparently one of the local winos. Their discussion, or rather, the monologue from the part of the social worker, aimed to convince the client to keep away from alcohol. I remember listening to their interaction with increasing astonishment, thinking: "Does she really think that this man is drinking because nobody has told him not to?"

Later, when I began to work as an organizational consultant, I discovered that the peculiar logic behind the social worker's action was common, not to say predominant, when it comes to organizational development and change. Here are some examples:

> A large company hired me to teach the managers how to perform appraisals and feedback dialogues. The reason was that both the managers and their subordinates were frustrated due to insufficient information exchange and poor contact during their encounters. When we discussed the design of the course, I found out that this would be the fourth course for this target group, with the same aim and basically the same content. My question to the personnel officer, who was my contact in the company, was: "If three courses haven't helped, what makes you think that a fourth one will?" It was reasonable to assume that the problem was not that the managers didn't know how to run these discussions. The problem was that they failed in spite of that knowledge.

The in-house leadership program in a company was composed of lectures about important things to consider when leading other people. Every part of the program was summarized into a checklist, and the lists were collected in a binder. The participants were supposed to go through the relevant list when they faced a difficult situation in their everyday leadership. As far as I know, nobody opened the binder after the course. That is as little a surprise as the fact that a car driver doesn't try to cope with a critical traffic situation by browsing through the driving school manual. What is surprising, though, is that the belief in this form of leadership development still is strong enough for them not to shut down the program.

An insurance company engaged a renowned management-consulting firm to map out what changes was necessary to increase efficiency and revenue. Their extensive report identified several areas of improvement, and pointed out necessary measures for each department to take. The report was spread and discussed throughout the company. A follow-up six months later showed that a few of the prescribed measures were carried out, but most of them were not. A closer scrutiny revealed that the report had unleashed an impressive creativity in finding argument for not following the recommendations. One of the excuses commonly used, was that circumstances had changed since the report were produced, thus making it obsolete. The same consulting firm was called in again to make a new study. The new report was practically a blueprint of the first one.

The examples above have several features in common. What stands out is that sensible thoughts are expressed in sensible plans, which are enacted in a sensible way, but without the result that the sensible thoughts had predicted. Like the social worker in the first example, the management consultants in the other examples wanted to attain behavioral change, and like her, they tried to bring about that by telling the clients what to do. This seemingly rational approach, which can be described in the term of *linear logic*, is repeatedly proven to be ineffective when it comes to changing complex phenomena, i.e. those who involve human beings in interaction with each other. Despite that, the leadership industry is quite successful in selling this kind of futile training programs again and again, even to the same company. The wish for matters to be uncomplicated and easy to grasp, paves the way for a huge market for simplifying methods, tools and interventions, with little impact on real issues.

This book, however, is not a "quick-fix" manual, filled with checklists and simplistic or facile advices. Rather, it demonstrates how to build a culture of openness and trust, and it shows the benefits of doing that work in terms of business efficiency and employee wellbeing. It does this by giving full justice to the complexity of human behavior, while making that complexity comprehensible to the average reader. To paraphrase Albert Einstein: my intention is to describe the dynamics of management team development as simple as possible, but not simpler.

Most people who work in teams have never experienced being part of a team that shares a profound level of openness and trust. Indeed, there remain those in business who would still recoil from applying these very words to a business setting. Yet, rather than enabling team members to exhibit their natural ingenuity and creativity, the team dynamic, instead, typically inhibits its members, rendering them cautious. So prevalent is this that, over time, we have taken for granted that cautiousness and defensiveness are merely intrinsic aspects of teams, and little or nothing can be done about that. "Good" teams are no exception; when a team is perceived as good by its members, that usually means the spirit is high and people enjoy coming together. However, it also means that each person operates under the premise that everyone will avoid issues that might upset other team members. For most team members, feeling comfortable and not losing face will be prioritized before accountability and excellent performance.

Not so in this book. Here, you will closely follow a fictitious top management team that is actually a composite of teams with whom I have worked many times in the recent past. By following this procedure, I've been able to pick clear examples of key elements of the process as the team journeys from mutual mistrust, defensiveness, and mediocre performance to profound feelings of togetherness, strong commitment, and excellent performance. The description of their step-by-step development process runs throughout the book, alternating with reasoning parts that shed light on the intra- and inter-personal dynamics. You will recognize most of the situations described from your own experiences as a team member, while the reasoning parts will help you understand the underlying driving forces behind the behaviors. You will also find strategies for dealing with them.

To accomplish this, the book intertwines real-time events with theoretical discussions throughout, in order to deepen the understanding of the behavior of the team members as it is occurring. It also brings the abstract theories behind what is occurring into flesh and bone at the same time, making it easier for you to apply these theories to situations you face all the time in your workaday life.

To distinguish these two streams, the first is written as a real-time narrative of the management team's development process as it occurs in a company "offsite" retreat over a period of three days. The real-time narrative can be summarized as a step-by-step evolution of the team as the members move from defensiveness, manipulations, and dysfunctional communications into a state of candor, commitment, and mutual accountability. The actual text of the narrative is distinguished by having narrower margins.

The second text consists of reflections on the course of events during the development process, which are built on theory as well as on my experience of developing management teams for the last 25 years. This text is distinguished by full margins.

Chapter 1 sets the framework for the development process by stressing the team members' responsibility for propelling it toward the goals they have previously agreed upon. Some of these are core themes that will be elaborated later in the book, including: role patterns and behavioral expectations as impediments for performance; how trying to simplify complex issues become part of the problem, not the solution; the importance of feedback; and how exposure and defensiveness affect team processes.

Chapter 2 gives a background of why the management team was in urgent need of improvement when the CEO brought in the consultant. Interviews conducted with individual team members in advance of the "offsite" revealed that the team's performance as a whole was impaired by several shortcomings: inefficient decision-making; decisions not carried out to full effect; lack of cooperation between departments, and lack of comprehensive overview; management's lack of credibility as a model for the rest of the company; and management's inability to deal with, or even discuss, any of the problems listed above.

Chapter 3 describes some of the defensive maneuvers management team members are using to avoid issues that might cause embarrassment or discomfort. These include: a maneuver named *He who sees the problem becomes the problem* and a*pparent matter-of-factness,* two defensive strategies designed to spare team members discomfort, but at the cost of effectively preventing root problems from being addressed, discussed, and solved. Another impediment to efficient problem-solving is described in this chapter: applying linear logic to non-linear problems, for example using a simple *A Causes B* formula for describing situations where, in fact, the elements affect each other reciprocally. Finally, a breakthrough in team communication occurs in this chapter, as one team member dares to reveal his true feelings. This is described and analyzed to illustrate the interdependence of openness and trust.

The first part of **Chapter 4** looks at how the management team members avoid accountability by using ambiguous communication. The second part returns to the discussion of feedback, introduced in Chapter 1, to distinguish *evaluative* and *personal feedback*, together with the consultant's strong recommendation to use personal feedback as a tool for improving team performance. Manipulative use of feedback, *i.e.*, when a person uses feedback to bully someone instead of helping him—a common tactic for getting the upper hand over another person and, at the same time, disguising doing so by pretending to be helpful—is also discussed.

The third part of this chapter focuses on pros and cons of using a management team as a decision tool, as compared to having the CEO make all decisions him or herself. The decision triangle—a theoretical framework for understanding under what circumstances speed, quality, or commitment should be prioritized in the decision process—is also described and discussed.

Chapter 5 gives an overview of Chris Argyris' theories of how defensive mechanisms in organizations are established and maintained. According to Argyris, much of our defensive behavior is a by-product of our social upbringing, i.e. us learning not to embarrass people by giving attention to less flattering aspects of their behavior. He uses the apt term *skilled incompetence* for this acquired inability to just tell it as it is. Teams of skilled incompetent members usually develop behavioral patterns— *defensive routines* in Argyris' terms—giving them a feeling of dealing with issues while, as a matter of fact, they are avoiding them. I use the term *Structural Solutions to Dynamic Problems* for one of the most common ways to give an impression of solving a problem without addressing the sensitive and potentially upsetting emotional aspects of it. For example, management might reorganize the company to avoid a conflict between two managers instead of just going to the bottom of their disagreement.

To fulfill its purpose, the act of covering up must itself be covered up; thus, it takes a lot of *fancy foot-work* to make the avoiding of core issues look as if it were acts of managerial wisdom. An inflated jargon and slogans devoid of obligations are ubiquitous in defensive organizations trying to look successful. In reality, though, avoiding unpleasant aspects of reality is no way to success; rather it paves the way for discouragement and mediocre performance.

However, the consequences of defensive mechanism in an organization can be more disastrous than so, which is dramatically demonstrated by the experience of the Challenger and Columbia space shuttle accidents. The excellent reports over the causes of these catastrophes are used to illustrate the potentially disastrous effects of a defensive organizational culture. A central point here is that applying structural — or technical — solutions to dynamic — or behavioral — problems was a main reason measures taken after the first accident were inadequate to prevent the second accident.

In **Chapter 6**, I'll introduce the core model for the team development process: *the LOT Helix*™ . Basically, it is a model for taking the team from a defensive level of social convenience to a sufficient level of openness and trust that enables them to address, discuss, and solve their most complex and sensitive issues. The level of openness and trust is correlated to different levels of management team functioning and to the team's ability to handle different degrees of complexity. Finally, I'll apply the theory of the LOT helix to the development of the management team we'll be following throughout the book. The way the development process has been conducted is explained as the team having to reach a deeper level of openness and trust if it is to be able to fulfill its duties.

Chapter 7 will sum up the three-day offsite team development process, as well as report actions and reactions the management team realizes afterward. Thus, you will "be present" as the outcome of the management team's development program begins to show both the company and individual benefits of their "offsite" activities, as well as how the commitment and enthusiasm developed between the members is spread all over the company. The key to this success is management team members addressing, discussing, and solving issues they previously swept under the rug. The profound openness and trust attained by the team during the offsite made it possible to discuss sensitive issues without fearing "loss of face" or "being stabbed in the back" for the first time in their history of working together. The real-life narrative of the progress of the management team show several examples of how this openness and trust promote behavior that benefits the company: assuming of responsibility, dealing with conflicts in a constructive way, and proactively addressing obstacles to company success.

A spin-off from the team development process—and, at the same time, proof of how profound the process has been—is the deepening of the participants' relations to their families and friends. Many of them reported that they were having more sincere talks with their spouses and children than ever before, or at least for many years.

This should not come as a surprise. Work-life and personal-life are communicating vessels. The straightjacket imposed on one's emotional life over years spent in a corporate climate which compels them to take a defensive stance to protect themselves, will, eventually, constrain their emotional vitality in the personal sphere as well. Correspondingly, the vitalization of work-life caused by the kind of team development process described here will spill over into the team members' personal lives. Therefore, the ability to build a sufficient level of openness and trust with their colleagues is not the only thing the team will take away from the offsite. The members will also gain individual competences that they can apply wherever they may need to, throughout their lives.

I don't expect that just reading this book will make the reader an expert on how to build an excellent team. However, my wish is that it will inspire to increase the awareness of what really affects performance, and also to mobilize the courage to do what is necessary for building a high-performance team culture. To accomplish that, I highly recommend the reader to transform insights from reading the book into action, for example to try out what happens when he or she shows just a little more openness than feels comfortable. This should of course be done with a good intention and with high attention and awareness of other people's reactions, not as a pretext to blurt out "truths" about others. My point here is that an insight not acted upon stays in a fantasy world to the benefit of nobody; on the contrary, it might just increase the knowing-doing gap that impede efficiency in so many organizations. On the other hand, taking action will lead to new insights, which will, in turn, trigger new actions, and so on, thus creating a process of change and true learning with the use of little effort. It merely will take the courage to "tell it as it is."

The Management Team

Richard – CEO
John – Marketing Manager
Mary – Manager Custom Relations
Jay – IT Manager (CIO)
Robert – Production Manager
Mark - Purchasing Manager
Victor – CFO
Susan – Personnel Manager
Jane – Administrative Manager

CHAPTER 1.
STARTING THE TEAM DEVELOPMENT PROCESS

The management team is gathered at a beautiful conference retreat, far away from the daily grind of the office. They are here to work on cooperation, efficiency, and "team-building" over the course of three late summer days. The atmosphere appears easy and relaxed, though the nervousness of some of the participants is apparent through their breezy façades. They are sitting on chairs arranged in a circle, and those who have brought folders or note-pads keep them in their laps, or beneath their chairs. All are gazing expectantly at the two consultants who have been hired to guide them through the three days ahead.

One of the consultants speaks: "First of all, I want to welcome you to this gathering," he begins. Then he briefly runs through the appointed times for lunch and dinner breaks, and other logistical details.

1

After a short break, the other consultant continues: "As you all know, we interviewed each of you a little over a week ago. We won't discuss those interviews in any detail here, because their purpose was not to enable us to run interference among you. Rather, we would like to share our overall impression of the management team, as it evolved from the interviews.

"What we found can be summed up in three points: (1) an insufficient sense of responsibility for the company as a whole; (2) an insufficient sense of responsibility for the implementation of decisions made by the management team; and (3) an insufficient sense of responsibility for making the management team an efficient executive forum. Since "responsibility" is the key word here, we want to invite you to use these three days as productively as possible to solve the problems inherent in your team's way of working.

"If we had to pick one critical tool in that solution, it could be each of you providing the team with the necessary feedback to develop efficiency, both within the group and in the company as a whole." He gestures to a flip board on the wall on which this task has been written.

After yet another brief pause, he continues. "Our role during these days is to help you see and understand what it is you do together and how that corresponds to the goals you have set for your company. We shall not be telling you what you should be doing differently. Figuring that out will be your job."

Why this framework?

Right from their introduction, the consultants articulate a framework for the meeting that rests on handing over the responsibility for the retreat to the participants. This means that everything the members of the management team do, or neglect to do, can be treated as an aspect of the team's competence. By choosing this method, the consultants aim to block an escape route that groups often like to use: blaming their shortcomings on circumstances beyond their own control.

You may ask yourself why the consultants would choose not to do what the team expects them to do, namely, to provide an analysis of their issues, along with an activity program designed to solve them. There are several good reasons for this:

1. As with most companies that have been operating for a while, this company—let's call it Company X—has, in the past, hired experts who have analyzed the company's deficiencies and prescribed measures to address them. As with many companies that have done this, the prescribed measures have not been implemented strongly enough to be effective in resolving the issues.

This lack of effectiveness can be ascribed to several things. First, no consultant, no matter how perceptive or talented, can develop the same deep understanding of conditions within an organization as can those who work for the company on a day-to-day basis. The advice and directives from an outsider will always be built on a limited understanding. In order to effect meaningful change, the consultant must, first, free the understanding the participants already possess. Only then can he add to it in order to lead the team to constructive action for the good of the organization.

2. Analyses of human systems usually remain too abstract to be useful as a foundation for concrete action. They can be so simplified that any prescribed actions will lack real effect. For example, one can turn a blind eye to the more complicated aspects of human interaction in favor of focusing on a single aspect that can be expressed in a simple cause-and-effect formula—that is to say, in terms of *linear logic*. In chapter 3, we shall address the implications of this way of looking at causation.

3. An analysis built on previously gathered data will, in all likelihood, be obsolete by the time it is presented. This is especially true when it describes complex human behavioral patterns. The potential for both understanding and change exists in the present—that is to say, in the precise moment in which a phenomenon, or a problem, reveals itself in the form of real actions and reactions among those involved. Once the moment has passed and the situation has dissipated, most of the complex information regarding the actual course of events will be lost. This is especially true of the emotional reactions of the

people involved; the immediate experience will soon be transformed into rationalizations and reconstructions that are often defined more by the need to sugar-coat or simplify reality than by what actually took place.

4. The phenomenon of *participation/ownership*. There is a higher likelihood that the team will emphatically take on the task of solving a problem if they feel ownership of both the understanding and the solution of that problem— that is, if they participate in the process from which the solution emerges. If someone outside the group articulates the issues and prescribes how they should be dealt with, there is an increased likelihood that the team members will reject the aspects of the analysis that they dislike, for one reason or another. This rejection will usually occur at the very point at which they are supposed to transform their understanding of the solution into concrete actions, if not sooner. Lack of participation/ownership is a common reason that ideas intended to bring about change fail to gain traction in practical reality.

5. The last and, perhaps, most important reason is that the consultants in this case have loftier ambitions than simply contributing to understanding. Their aim is to help participants develop their own competence when it comes to in-depth problem-solving in the company, rather than simply ameliorating the symptoms for problems as they arise. This means, to paraphrase an old Confucian adage, they aim not to serve fish to the management team, but rather to teach the team how to fish. A precondition for teaching this is developing their ability to insure quality

in their own work process. What this means in practice will become clear to you as you continue to read this book. In the meantime, let us return to our management group.

Around the circle, there is confused silence. John, head of marketing, wonders, "What are we supposed to do, in more concrete terms?" Victor, head of finance, turns to the consultant who last spoke. "You're the experts here. Where do you think we should start?" Once again, the consultants point to the group's own responsibility for dealing with their issues.

In the absence of help or advice, anxiety levels in the group rise further. Jane, head of administration, begins to rifle through her papers. Victor crosses his arms and looks pointedly out the window. John begins talking about how goal-oriented he is and how he dislikes hokey consultants who do not present clear goals. The rest look like they are grasping for clues in what has already been said.

After a while, Richard, the company CEO, speaks. "Okay, let's see if we can structure the task." He goes up to the flip board on the wall. "I suggest we do a brainstorming exercise. Give me suggestions for things we need to change."

Richard's initiative is met with approval, and the team quickly comes up with a dozen points they need to deal with. These span a broad range, from strategically important issues to small annoyances in daily operations.

"This looks good," says Richard. "What should we do to solve these problems?" Another page is filled with proposed fixes. The team is working with notable efficiency and not without enthusiasm.

Mary, who is head of customer service, has been quiet for a while. Now, she says, "Wait a minute, this list looks familiar. Aren't these the exact same points that were raised at the conference a little less than a year ago?"

There is a brief silence, but then the work continues as if nothing was said. After a while, one of the consultants interrupts the conversation and turns to Mary. "How do you feel about the reaction to your comment?" She answers, somewhat apologetically, that she did not get an answer, but that she had not really expected one, either. Jay, head of the IT department, continues his previous exposition about how to expand tech support. Robert, head of production, joins in with a general comment on how the tech department is vital to the company.

The consultant turns to Mary again. "You're still not getting an answer." Jay is visibly annoyed. "Actually, I think we were doing a good job, and Mary's comment didn't further the discussion one iota. We were supposed to take responsibility for this ourselves, and now the two of you are distracting us with your comments." Mark, the sales manager, agrees and adds, addressing the consultant, "What do you want from us?"

The consultant persists and turns to Jay. "Is she wrong about what she's saying, or do you also recognize this list from the last conference?" Jay reluctantly agrees that he does recognize the list, yet he continues to argue that they ought to be allowed to keep working at solving the problems, rather than getting hung up on Mary's comments.

"But isn't it interesting to ask why the problems haven't been solved if you identified them a year ago?" the consultant asks. "Plus, what are you doing now that's so different from what you were doing then? What makes you more likely to solve them this time?"

The team is now divided into two camps. Victor, head of finances, and Susan, head of HR, feel that Mary has a point, and they think they should discuss why they did not implement the fixes from the last conference. Jay, Robert, Mark, and John want to continue working on the list. Richard tries to stay neutral and says nothing. Jane, head of administration, does not say anything either, as her role in the team is usually limited to agreeing with Richard and supporting his suggestions.

Role patterns and behavioral expectations

At this point, an important detail of the exploratory method on which the consultants are basing their approach is revealed. If they had laid out a structure for how the team should tackle their development, the repetitive and inefficient pattern in their approach would not have come to light—nor would the members of the team have had to reflect on the fact that they were doing something they knew from experience would not produce results. Even if the unhelpful pattern *had* come to light, they could easily have blamed it on the guidance of the consultants. Instead, everything that happens from this point on will show how each one of them, as well as the team as a whole, tackles their shared reality.

The insecurity and frustration the team members express when they are supposed to be working on their development process is, in some ways, understandable. The task they have been presented with puts them in a situation that is reminiscent of many others they have not been able to handle in their day-to-day business dealings in the past, situations that they have avoided at any cost.

While the goal of their task is clearly articulated, it is also abstract. The roadmap, in the form of concrete actions, is not yet visible. The team members have neither experience nor a method for dealing with the dynamic inherent in their own workflow in a conscious and goal-oriented way—a precondition for successfully completing the task.

Moreover, the roles and patterns that the management team has developed throughout the course of its existence are not helping them succeed at the present task. Team members are part of the team because they each fulfill a certain functional role within the company and, to some extent, because of their individual knowledge and leadership qualities. Management issues are normally dealt with by those whose positions they most concern on an operational level, in conjunction with others who may be needed to contribute their particular expertise.

Their day-to-day discussions tend to be characterized by a formal hierarchy of power, as well as an informal power struggle of which the participants are only partially conscious. Several team members have developed hidden means of exerting power, for example, by withholding or distorting information, forging alliances, and/or ignoring input from others. Since the task at this retreat demands true and complete information from all the participants in order to be accomplished in a meaningful way, the old roles and behaviors can only be obstacles; they can never help here.

Additionally, a role is usually defined as a set of expected behaviors, such as executing formalized tasks that might be expressed in a job description. In this retreat, however, the formal role prescribes a course of action that is independent of any individual team member.

Here, we are more interested in the informal roles that result from the team members ascribing qualities to one another. These informal roles are maintained by the individuals as they receive affirmation for behaving in accordance with what the others expect of them. Of course, the obverse is also true: they will be ignored when they do not behave accordingly.

Thus, the role patterns—the patterns formed by these interacting roles—have a normative function: they regulate what may be said and done and who may say and do it. By adhering to their informal roles, team members can avoid uncertainty and overt power struggles. They can also keep others from seeing sides of themselves they would prefer not be seen. The emotional security offered by an established set of roles leads the team members to fight to maintain it, even when maintaining these roles obviously does not contribute to the success of the team.

Instead of embracing that which is new and uncertain in a given situation, the team reaches for a familiar approach that lets them act according to the assigned roles they know well—in this case, listing problems and solutions. Richard takes the helm by virtue of his comfort with formal leadership, letting others join in as they choose. The wish of the team members to be on familiar ground is so great that the astute insight brought up by Mary—*i.e.*, that this same approach has not led to change in the past—is vigorously rejected.

This episode clearly illustrates that team members' emotional needs can quickly become more important to them than results—a fact that is obscured by an ostensibly goal-oriented approach. The strategically important job of making the management team more efficient is

transformed into an operational task. Attempts to ele-
vate the discussion to the level of strategizing for problem-solving are forcefully rejected. Here, too, we see
the team exposing one of its core problems, as well as
the defensive dynamic that prevents the members from
solving it.

Complexity or Simplification

Another shortcoming of the management team is its
difficulties in dealing with complexity. Issues that
involve overarching responsibility, implementation of
strategy, and their ability to cooperate all involve complex dynamic sequences of events that are difficult or
impossible for them to take in fully. Instead of exploring
the complex dynamic behind the group's failures, they
rearticulate the problem in terms of the simple logic of
the problem-solution.

In *Change*, the authors describe how "the terrible sim-
plifications" can become obstacles to effecting change.[2]
By reducing a problem we cannot grasp to one we can
understand, we achieve a sense of control. However, the
actions that seem easy and natural according to this simplified understanding rarely solve the real problem.

Our management team attempted to solve their problems with an action plan in the past and should, therefore,
have known that it would not work. Yet, this insight did

---

[2] Watzlawick, P., Weakland, J., and Fish, R., *Change: Principles of Problem
Formation and Problem Resolution* (New York: W.W. Norton & Co., 1974).

not gain traction with the team, not even when the simple truth was blatantly articulated by a team member. The need to solve the task in an effective way was crowded out by the even stronger need for control, safety, and preservation of self-image.

The need for control is expressed in team members' thoughts and words, but it is the need for self-preservation that actually shapes their actions. They are unable to see how they, both as individuals and as a team, actually maintain the problems they are trying to solve. As is the case with most of us, their upbringing and social experiences honed the type of incompetence[3] that made them blind to the underlying issues going on within the group. At this point, the team's inability to see what is readily apparent between them instead prompts them to seek to avoid conflict, and to keep those less flattering aspects of themselves from being brought to light and examined. The price of this "peace of mind," however, is that they become prisoners of the group dynamic.

The tug-of-war over how the group should proceed has ground things to a halt. Those who want to keep working on the action plan make a few attempts that flounder because the others fail to respond to their words. Those who question the work cannot present sufficiently concrete alternatives to satisfy

---

[3] The American organizational psychologist Chris Agryris coined the term "skilled incompetence," meaning roughly "learned incompetence." See Overcoming Organizational Defenses (Needham Heights, MA: Allyn and Bacon, 1990), whose theory is explained in detail in chapter 5.

the increasingly irritated demands of the rest. In the silence that eventually prevails, one of the consultants reminds them of the task it was given. "What feedback would you give each other based on how the work has gone so far?" he asks.

Instead of following the implicit invitation to give each other feedback, the team members engage in a discussion of the meaning of the word "feedback." Susan, head of HR, says she has learned that one should offer positive feedback first, so that the recipient is receptive to the negative. John maintains there is an open enough attitude among the team members for everyone to voice an opinion about the others, but it feels odd to do so on command. Jay agrees with John and adds, "I've already told the others what I think of what they do." Jane agrees that it is easy to give positive feedback, but harder to voice negatives. "One doesn't want to hurt anyone," she offers. However, when Jane is encouraged to give positive feedback to someone on the team, she cannot think of anything to say. "It would feel unnatural in this situation," she says. When asked about the last time she has given any of the others positive feedback, she is forced to admit that she might not have done that very often. Nor could she answer the consultant's follow-up question, why she felt it was easier to voice positive feedback. Victor tried to come to her rescue by saying that she is always friendly to him, but nobody is interested in further developing the discussion about Jane's ability to give feedback.

Instead, Jay poses the question, "How can one know if feedback contributes to developing efficiency within the company?" When none of the participants answer him, he looks to the consultants. There is no answer from that corner either.

At that point, Jay leads the conversation to the issue of how to act to insure optimal communication with subordinate managers and co-workers. Robert and Jane pick up that line of discussion with some sweeping examples of how it would be hard to get the time to speak to others in the company.

One of the consultants points out that they are talking about feedback but not giving any. Jay quickly jumps in. "I have some feedback for you, Susan. I think you manage the absence statistics better now than you did this spring." Susan thanks him for the feedback. The others get quiet, as if they are searching their memories for something pertinent to say. After a short while, they are back to their former discussion of what the term "feedback" really means and the risks inherent in being open with each other.

The Importance of Feedback

As the consultants predicted, the seemingly benign task of giving each other feedback actually constituted a threat to their equilibrium. Like most groups, both inside and out of the workplace, the management team followed an unwritten rule: *Don't give your workmates personal feedback, especially not if you suspect they won't like what you have to say.*

In general, the realization that giving one another honest feedback is necessary, combined with the uncertainty about how honest one should actually dare to be, creates a dilemma for most of us. To escape this, we often rationalize—that is to say, we come up with seemingly reasonable explanations as to why it is unnecessary, or inappropriate, to speak our minds. A common excuse is that we do not have anything to say that has not already been said.

This is almost never true. Victor and John can have lengthy discussions about how Richard operates as a CEO without Richard being present. Richard and Victor can agree that John can be pushy and square at management team meetings, but nobody has relayed this to John.

When it is brought to their attention that they avoid giving feedback, the team members insist on ostensibly rational explanations. "We don't want to get too personal; the management team meetings are meant for business issues," or "It's risky to be too open with what you think; you might jeopardize the cordial atmosphere within the company." While it is not difficult to prove the hollowness of these arguments, they are still common, not just within Company X but in most organizations. This can be attributed to the fact that they serve an important emotional need: the need for avoiding unpleasant confrontation.

In reality, a qualitative and well-developed system of feedback is of vital importance for any organization to run efficiently in a changing world. For it to be qualitative, feedback must not be watered down or made impersonal, nor can it avoid what can be perceived by the receiver as unpleasant. For it to be well-developed, it needs to be a natural part of all interactions at every level of the organization.

Different types of institutionalized feedback, such as appraisals or monthly meetings, will not suffice. The most effective feedback is given in immediate response to an individual's actions. This necessitates that the atmosphere within the company be open and trusting, so that the speaker will have no need to guard his or her tongue for fear of any consequences. Even so, each person also needs to possess individual courage.

The fear of giving feedback is not just about a fear of hurting someone, or fear of retribution. There can also be a fear of the *intimacy* that arises when people show clearly that they are reacting to each other. In close relationships, we have less control over what we show of ourselves, which increases the risk of our being confronted with unpleasant truths that can be unsettling to our self-image. In a business setting, that same fear makes us want to set up rules for feedback, such as the one Susan referred to, that is, offering positive feedback first.

Feedback serves three important functions:

1. It provides the individual an opportunity to learn, grow, develop, and orient herself in daily life. Honest feedback provides information on how individuals affect their surroundings. By comparison, lack of feedback isolates people, denying them realistic contact with a situation and thus lessening their ability to affect it. Instead, they are left to their own fantasies, which then serve as motivation for their actions as well as the basis for their own self-image. This makes for a fragility that can have a negative impact on mental health over time.

2. Feedback contributes to vitality and drive within the team. When the members of the team give one another feedback on how they perceive each other's influence inside and outside the team, they uncover hidden blockages in the dynamics and obstacles to efficient work. Feedback insures that the team has enough depth of process to solve their tasks. (For a definition of "depth of process," see chapter 6.)

3. Feedback is an invaluable instrument for *the organization*. Most organizations today are run on vision, values, and information, which leaves a wide berth for individual interpretations based on individual needs. It is not enough for management to communicate their goals and visions; they must also put in place dynamic systems that maintain these and transform them into useful actions. A necessary

element of any dynamic system is to insure that members of the organization receive continuous feedback about whether or not their actions are in line with company goals. This is true not only for the typical sorts of actions one usually notices and measures, but also for the thousands of small, daily actions that contribute to the support of the organization's culture.

A critically important element in the effort of team leaders to increase their ability to exert quality control on their own team will thus be the development of a vital and well-functioning system of feedback. The effects of this will not just benefit the management team. The ability of the team members to provide feedback will enable them to work toward increased openness within the entire organization in a trustworthy way.

Exposure and Defensiveness

Thus far in the developmental process of our management team, we have been able to see a number of factors that limit the team's ability to handle change and complexity: a tendency to oversimplify, stereotypical role behavior, lack of feedback, and superficial and conciliatory behavior among team members.

So far, the consultants have made no serious attempts to get the team to change their ways. Their purpose, as stated earlier (p. 2), is to expose the team's way of working so that it becomes painfully obvious to the members. An intellectual understanding of the difficulties has proven insufficient as a means of effecting change. Emotional motivation is necessary for team members to grapple with the problems with sufficient force. By increasing their awareness of the causes of their frustrations during their attempt at cooperation, the consultants hope to bring about this emotional motivation.

The members of the management team have shown sides of themselves that typify their way of reacting in situations that are marked by a high degree of uncertainty. For example, there is Richard's habit of hiding behind his traditional leadership role; John's angry demands for action when he feels he is losing control of a situation; Jay's slightly manic tech jargon; and Victor's way of first pointedly retreating and then attempting to place responsibility for the team's predicament outside of himself—in this case, on the consultants.

In a similar way, each member reveals his or her own particular defense mechanisms, manipulative tactics, self-imposed restraints, and other personality traits that characterize the ways in which they handle the situation. The other members register this—at this point mainly on a subconscious level—and as the process continues, each person's contribution to the group dynamic will become increasingly overt. This, in combination with an improvement in the quality of mutual feedback, will create a beneficial atmosphere for individual and organizational learning.

We have also seen a number of defensive reactions that have exposed certain deficiencies of the group as a whole: offloading responsibility onto others (projection), ignoring what is happening (denial), and providing seemingly reasonable explanations (rationalization). We humans use defensive mechanisms to maintain our self-image in situations in which we feel threatened. All psychological defensive mechanisms have in common that they create blinders to the aspects of ourselves that we would rather not see. This could be our powerlessness, incompetence, cowardice, insidiousness, or other such "forbidden" qualities.

The downside of these defensive tactics is that they also contribute to maintaining our inability to deal with a situation in a useful way. For instance, if we can blame a problem on someone else, we have no reason to do anything to solve it. The same thing happens if we come up with good explanations as to why there really is no problem, despite plenty of signals from the surrounding environment to the contrary.

In addition, defensive tactics lead to manipulative behaviors: someone who does not openly face and accept their shortcomings has a tendency to employ various maneuvers to disguise or hide them from others. In short, defense mechanisms contribute to making us less understandable to one another. Appendix A describes psychological defense mechanisms that are relevant to understanding human dynamics in groups and organizations.

To show how the learning process of the management team connects with their daily managerial work, we shall now take a closer look at the situation at Company X and what its management team looked at the outset of their development process.

CHAPTER 2.
THE SITUATION AT THE OUTSET OF THE DEVELOPMENT PROCESS

In the first chapter, we were thrown right into the off-site development process of the management team. Now let's look back at the situation at the outset of that process, to see what put the team and the company in the situation with which they are now struggling to cope.

History of Company X

With 250 employees, Company X is a fairly typical mid-sized company. It was formed in the late 1980s, when a larger company spun off part of its business.

At the beginning, the former mother company was Company X's only customer, providing it with a sheltered market for its products. This symbiotic relationship between the two companies meant that the spin-off only changed things on paper. The routines that had been in place when the companies were connected continued to work successfully under the new circumstances as well.

After a few years, however, the former mother company began to turn to other suppliers for the services offered by Company X, which forced Company X to seek more customers. As a result, it hired sales people assigned to each of its production departments. It also made cautious overtures to the competitors of the former mother company, which proved unsuccessful. The creation of a few new products forged some new customer relationships, but only to a small extent, and not enough to compensate for the business lost.

The years of advantage had shaped the business mindset and culture of Company X. The increased competition, with the accompanying new need to market its services both to new and old customers, did not change the ingrained company culture to any significant extent. For a long time, the management refused to see the discrepancy between the new business logic and the old ways of running things. With time, however, it became increasingly obvious that the company could not remain competitive being run the way it was. A common issue in discussions among managers was their difficulty in getting employees to take initiative in line with updated company goals and strategies.

At this point, the management team gathered the entire staff and presented them with the company's vision: to make Company X a leader in its field, in competition with other players. They also presented a number of concrete areas for improvement: more flexibility, delegation of more responsibilities to those who were in direct contact with customers; and, in general, an increased understanding of the realities of business throughout the company.

This was a partial success: everyone seemed to understand and to like the new strategy. However, in terms of action, the results were negligible. After a short period of increased vitality and faith in the future, the employees of Company X went back to their old ways of working.

This became apparent in various ways in subsequent management team meetings, and management was soon forced to realize that the desired shifts in attitude and behavior had not succeeded as they had hoped. Ultimately, they conducted an organizational inventory, with the help of external experts, which led to a complete reorganization of the company. Marketing and customer support were emphasized as areas of priority and given their own departments. Those who had previously been on the management team in the capacity of product managers now found themselves working under a head of production. At first, this generated some discontent, but everyone soon accepted the change.

However, while management found that the change of the organizational structure had been successful, they soon realized that the expected shifts in attitude and behavior were barely perceptible. Nor was there any improvement in terms of results. Company X lost a few customers and lost bids for new prospective clients to competitors who they generally perceived as delivering services that were inferior to their own. On top of all this, several key players who had been recruited to strengthen the company's focus had quit when it became apparent that the company had not lived up to the pretty words in its mission statement.

The production and marketing departments blamed each other, and both blamed management, for the failure. Customer support blamed marketing for not using their expertise in sales, and also blamed management. Staff personnel complained about the lack of cooperation between departments and blamed this on management as well.

When the issue of lost business was raised in the management team, the discussion developed along two lines of thought. One line pointed to unfortunate circumstances as strongly contributing to the failure: the economy, problems with suppliers, the business practices of competitors, and just plain bad luck were blamed. The other line involved the staff's inability to understand the intentions of the management team. Regardless of which of the two lines was in focus, the discussion inevitably ground to a halt and shifted to dealing with concrete daily operational issues instead.

The inability to deal with issues that everyone saw as central to the development of the company led to frustration, which eventually turned into discouragement and resignation. At this point, a member of the board recommended the CEO engage a couple of consultants who were renowned for successfully pushing management teams in the right direction. After a long and intense discussion with the management team, the CEO decided to meet with the consultants recommended to him, to find out what they might be able to do about the situation. Since the consultants referred to worked under my supervision, I had good insight throughout the development process.

When the consultants met with the management team, they soon saw that the change in attitude and behavior that everyone professed to want had not taken hold there. To be sure, no one openly opposed the new strategy, but when it was concretized in the form of actions and decisions, several people on the team came up with "factual" objections or were noticeably passive. As a result, the enthusiasm that was needed to lend credibility to the management's vision was absent.

Individual team members felt free to interpret the decisions in ways that benefited their own interests. When the consultants pointed this out, they were met with total denial from the entire management team. Everyone claimed they fully supported the changes in the company and thought their actions were in its best interests. However, they did feel that the team itself could be more efficient, especially when it came to making and enforcing decisions.

The discussion led to the management team proposing that the consultants should help them strengthen their team and improve communication between individual members. The consultants responded that, while the task was clearly delineated, communication and team-building were means, rather than a goal, for the management team. In the end, they agreed to work with the team to develop its ability to implement—that is to say, to bring about necessary changes within the organization.

The Situation at the Outset

In anticipation of their work with the management team, the consultants interviewed each of the participants individually. Their purpose was twofold: first, to gather as much relevant information as possible about the company, and second, to begin building the cooperative partnership with each person that would be necessary to effect change. For the members of the management team, the interviews were also an opportunity to reflect on how the management of the company worked, and the ways in which they felt they had contributed to its successes and challenges.

In a company facing issues, one might expect that insight into the gravity of the situation and opinions on how to improve would vary from manager to manager. This was not at all the case with Company X. Each of the interviewees painted more or less the same picture of what the problems were and what needed to be done. They also all had difficulty seeing how they, themselves, had contributed to the issues, and to the fact that these issues had remained unresolved.

Nor did any one of them give a clear picture of how they had cooperated as a team. Rather, they described their roles in the chain of command, that is to say, their duties, powers, and areas of responsibility, but they could not say why their work often felt heavy and uninspired. Instead, they used mystifying circumlocutions, such as, "It's just in the atmosphere" or, "It's as if we're all hit by mental paralysis. The sky is the limit when we work in pairs, but when we work as a management team our ability to think evaporates completely." Someone said, "We can be in agreement at the meeting, but afterward I'm often unsure of what it was we agreed to."

Thus, several problem areas for the management team, as well as for the company in general, emerged over the course of the interviews. The most significant were:

Inefficient decision-making; Decisions are not implemented to full effect; Lack of cooperation between departments, and lack of comprehensive overview; Management lacks credibility as a model for the rest of the company; and The management team did not discuss any of these issues.

Inefficient decision-making

All interviewees expressed frustration with the management team's apparent inability to reach decisions within a reasonable time frame. This was especially true in the case of overarching strategic issues that spanned several departments. Easy operational decisions were made quickly: the head of a department would explain the conditions and the CEO would then declare his opinion on what to do in each situation. Usually, his suggestions were accepted with no further discussion. Issues concerning two departments could also be dealt with relatively quickly, though the decided actions were often in the nature of quick-fixes that did not solve the real problems — issues that were assumed to be settled had a tendency to show up on the agenda again and again (see below).

Moreover, complicated issues, such as enforcing change, were often subject to endless discussions that led to decisions being made without the proper support of all the team members. While everyone was relieved that a decision had been made, there was often uncertainty regarding what exactly had been decided. Many people also felt that the team dealt with so-called "bike rack issues"[4] rather than using its time for more important matters. A proposal was made that half the time be spent on operational issues and the other half on strategic planning. This proposal petered out because the group frequently "forgot" to shift focus until only a few minutes of the meeting remained.

---

[4] The expression comes from Parkinson's Law, which says that a management team can make a $10 million decision in 15 minutes but will spend hours discussing whether or not there should be a bike rack outside headquarters. The reason for this is that everyone can understand and relate to the "bike-rack" issue, but the $10 million issue might be too complicated for everyone to give input. Parkinson, Cyril Northcote, *Parkinson's Law — and other studies in administration*, third ed. (Boston: Houghton Mifflin Company, 1957), pp. 29–30.

Decisions are not implemented to full effect

One typical phenomenon at team meetings was that issues on which the team had previously made unanimous decisions were being raised again at subsequent meetings. This tended to cause irritation: "We agreed we'd do it this way. Why is this on the agenda again?" It often turned out that these decisions had only been partially implemented, or sometimes had not been implemented at all. This was attributed mainly to three things: (1) new facts had come to light that had made the implementation of the decision less wise; (2) resistance and lack of understanding from lower managers and co-workers had impeded the process; and (3) there was a widespread uncertainty among leaders and co-workers about how to transform the decisions into actions.

Lack of power to implement in these cases led the team into a downward spiral. The team's faith in its own decision-making abilities was weakened, which caused an air of despondency to permeate management meetings. It was as if no one really believed that the decisions would ever be implemented. This in turn led many to withhold information that threatened to complicate the decision-making process—but which would also have had the potential to improve the quality of it. The combination of lack of faith and badly substantiated decisions made the situation deteriorate further.

Lack of cooperation between departments and lack of comprehensive overview

A comprehensive organizational overview performed six months earlier pointed out several synergistic gains that would be possible if departments increased their cooperation. For instance, several staff functions were replicated in each department, which led to duplication of work, and also to no one taking responsibility for interdepartmental issues. An example of this was that every department had a different way of using its own tech support, thereby foreclosing any benefits that might be realized by the implementation of a company-wide system. This had been pointed out in the overview as a case that should urgently be dealt with, but the interviews revealed that no action had been taken yet.

A more serious matter was the lack of coordination on issues directly concerning the company's core business. The production department ignored the feedback that sales and customer support picked up in their interactions with customers. For their parts, the sales people were disinclined to involve the two other departments to enhance the presentation of the company's services and products. Indeed, in the interviews, the term "watertight compartments" was used to describe the relationship between departments.

This was largely a result of department managers not being able to cooperate in a constructive way. It was obvious that they were each guarding their own territory, even when doing so had negative consequences for the company as a whole. Everyone seemed to see that the others built walls around their own departments, but they regarded themselves as willing to cooperate. They all felt that the others did not understand the unique conditions for their departments.

One of the managers described the dynamics behind the disintegration of the decision-making process this way: "We agree on the overarching vision, but the more we break it down into goals, priorities, and actions, the less agreement there is within the team." This can be interpreted in the following way: The more concrete the issues become, the more clearly they collide with people's own power struggles, ambitions, and emotional needs. The hidden rivalry within the management team made it possible to discuss comprehensive visions as well as concrete operational issues, but not the strategy that tied them together.

Management lacks credibility as a model for the rest of the company

Another factor that contributed to the vicious circle the management team was caught in was this: their credibility was diminished in the eyes of the rest of the organization. The resistance to change shown by low-level managers and co-workers was strengthened by the fact that the signals they received from top management were vague, contradictory, and lacked the force that comes from enthusiasm and decisiveness. Many of the managers postponed the implementation of directives that came from their superiors until they could determine if there really was a reason to take them seriously. The lack of any sort of backup in the form of action from their most immediate supervisors often led them to conclude there was no such reason, and that made it completely legitimate to ignore such directives, as long as they could articulate a good explanation for why doing so was the wisest course of action. The most common explanations were that "those above" them did not understand the conditions for the practical work "on the ground," and that the old way of doing things had been successful so far, in any case. The validity of these claims was never actually checked out, of course, since they were merely specious arguments used to avoid responsibility. In reality, the problem was a reluctance to deal with the challenges and unpleasantness that change might bring.

The result of this attitude was that the efforts toward change usually ground to a halt, and management was spoken of throughout the company in condescending terms, as if it was something floating in the air with no connection to reality. At the same time, however, no one directly criticized his or her own manager, or the company CEO. Criticism was leveled in a more nebulous manner, at the management team as a whole.

The management team did not discuss any of these issues

Despite all the members of the management team being aware of these problems, there was no real discussion of them in management meetings. While there were many reactions to things that were not working, these did not lead to any comprehensive discussion of how cooperation worked, either in fact or as a new possibility. Instead, the factual aspects of what had gone wrong were rehashed over and over again. None of the managers had any answers to why the team's workflow was not placed under a magnifying glass. Basically, they were embarrassed if and whenever the question was raised.

Positive Aspects of Company X

The focus on the company's difficulties should not be allowed to obscure the positive aspects of management and the company's culture. The business was carried by the palpable pride that most employees took in their trade and by their sense of loyalty to the mission statement. Many were happy with their jobs as long as they got to work without too much interference. There was also a strong desire for employees on every echelon to ride out the storm and succeed. The atmosphere at work was, for the most part, friendly and marked by a sense of mutual appreciation and care. Management took pains to show respect for the competence of the employees, as well as for each other. There was a great deal of tolerance for the individual wishes of employees when it came to hours and other working conditions. Key figures for mental health indicated that Company X did well in comparison to similar companies.

Summary of the management team's situation

In general, Company X found itself in a situation in which conditions in the outside world were changing faster than the company itself. This is a classic problem, especially for companies that have existed in a relatively sheltered market, but it also applies to those who have seen business conditions change with increasing speed.

During the years of a more placid market, the company developed values, attitudes, and stances as well as implicit and explicit norms that were adapted to the situations at hand. Along with more formalized rules and routines, this created a *company culture* that was reasonably functional.

With increased competition, certain aspects of this culture began to limit efficiency. The changes management made were directed at structures and systems within the company. When these did not lead to the desired changes in patterns of thought and action, attempts were made to create a new company culture. Management relied on the aid of informational meetings and "kick-off"-type activities to address this, but the accustomed patterns resisted all of their attempts.

Much like most humans, companies are fundamentally unwilling to change unless they are forced to do so by circumstances, and even then they usually drag their heels. Resistance to change is generally due, among other things, to our having invested energy in adapting to the current situation, and thus tending to guard our investment. We are also good at giving ourselves advantages, even in a situation that is less than optimal. Many of us will build little enclaves of space for independent action within the framework of the organization and are unwilling to surrender the perceived power and freedom that these provide.

Within Company X, one could see several groups and individuals who had given themselves freedom from involvement in a way that obstructed cooperation with the rest of the business. The top management team members were no exception in that respect. They had built substantial walls between their departments, trying to minimize involvement from each other and from the rest of the organization. There were also a few people at the staff level who had developed special interests within their fields. No one really understood what it was they did, but they were allowed to keep at it, as everyone assumed it was important to the company. The unofficial—and real—reason was that no one was actually interested in achieving transparency about the degree to which the work was ruled by individual needs at the expense of the company's best interest. The risk that the searchlights would end up on one's own activities was enough of a deterrent against transparency.

The management team possessed the insight that change was necessary, but they were not able to disseminate this notion of change successfully throughout the organization. A great deal of effort was spent informing everyone about the new situation. Time was set aside across the entire company to give everyone a chance to discuss what this meant for their own tasks. Despite this effort, though, there was little change evident in the day-to-day work of the company—and in its profits.

Discrepancy between words and actions

A considerable contributing factor to the lack of efficiency in the effort to change the operation and culture of Company X was the discrepancy between words and actions. Like many in the vision-fueled companies of today, Company X's management fell prey to a verbal magic: they sought the "right" visionary phrases that would magically turn the company in the desired direction. This faith in the power of verbal messages contributed to a widespread inability to decode the non-verbal "messages" expressed in action, thus making it possible for anyone in the company to act against visions and policies without being arrested as long as they complied with them verbally. Consequently, many operational decisions and actions were actually based on values rooted in the old culture which, in more or less subtle ways, counteracted the new culture that management wanted to implement.

Of course, it would not have been impossible for the people on the management team to discover this gap between words and actions for themselves. Several of them provided many examples of it in their interviews. Despite this, the gap did not become a theme in management team discussions. Two main reasons for this were indicated during the interviews: (1) lack of attention; and (2) personal advantages of, or benefits from, not seeing.

Lack of attention

The realization that the behavior on the part of management did not always promote the desired culture only arose after the fact—that is to say, once the effects of the behavior became obvious, or when someone pointed them out. In the moment it happened, it was rarely noticed, not by the person performing the behavior nor by any managerial colleagues around him or her.

The reason for this may be that we are all trained to focus on concrete issues and the physical reality around us. Few of us have ever received any systematic training in seeing the more subtle effects that our actions have on other people.

Many managers pride themselves on being factual and analytical. However, these good qualities can become obstacles to seeing other aspects of what is going on. It is not unusual for signs that a decision will not be implemented to become visible during the decision-making process itself. This could take the form of opposition being expressed passively, or of those who are actually enthusiastic holding back for tactical reasons, or of a lack of appreciation on everyone's part for anyone else's input. All these behaviors lower commitment to implementing the decision, which also provides an excuse for sabotaging it.

Paying attention is undoubtedly the action of an individual, but in a group that exists over a long period of time, it is intimately linked to the degree of openness, trust, and personal intimacy existing between group members. We pay much attention to signals from people who are close, and therefore important to us; this sense of closeness is maintained by our continuously giving feedback on these signals, with or without words. Feedback, in turn, increases attention, which makes more feedback possible, and so on. We see more of the other person, while we show more of ourselves. This is what fuels a close relationship.

Using the language of information technology, one could express this process of building channels of communication as "increasing bandwidth," where the definition of "bandwidth" is the amount of information transferred per unit of time. The difference, when talking about humans, as opposed to technology, is that while the capacity of the cable company's network is defined at the outset, when it is dug into the ground, the bandwidth in human relationships and informational systems needs to be constantly, actively maintained. This demands both the courage to be open and clear about what you really think, as well as the ability to be receptive to the subtle signals sent by those around you.

Another aspect of the bandwidth in human systems is that we lose our ability to take in large amounts of relevant data when we become analytical and controlled. It is a well-known fact that only a small part of the information we receive through our senses is dealt with consciously. This explains why our logical models of dynamic inter-personal activities become so depleted of information. If we could permit ourselves to be fully immersed in the present, we would then open the mental channels that help us subconsciously read an immeasurably larger amount of relevant data than we could ever consciously perceive.

Lack of attention can reach nearly comic levels at times. One management team, which I coached (not at Company X), was discussing the importance of listening attentively to what each person said. One of the participants was completely absorbed in a business publication and did not take part in the conversation. I waited to see how long they could discuss this issue without shifting their attention to what was happening in the present: a person illustrating the issue by doing exactly what everyone else was agreeing they should not do.

For a long while, the discussion continued as if this person was not even in the room. When I finally drew their attention to him, it turned out that they had all noted his lack of engagement, but not the obvious contradiction between the norm that they were articulating verbally and that which their lack of reaction to the magazine-reader expressed. Neither had anybody considered the opportunity to use what was happening to anchor the discussion in reality. This learned lack of attention ("skilled incompetence" in the terminology of Chris Argyris; see chapter

5) proved to be based on a fear that the magazine-reader would be offended if his behavior came under scrutiny. Nobody wanted to take on the role of "judging" (their own expression) a co-worker, as no one was certain he or she was any better. This brings us to the next reason for the discrepancy between words and actions.

Benefits of not seeing

When an organization is plagued by behaviors that do not serve its business interests, it is easy to assume that many have something to gain from letting things remain as they are. In individual psychology, the term "primary gain" is used to denote the "advantages" that a person gains from his symptoms: the sympathy of the people around him, lessened demands, amelioration of his own sense of guilt, etc. In the treatment of individual neuroses, the primary gain is a powerful source of resistance. In the same way, resistance to organizational changes is usually tied to the things the members gain from having things remain the same.

The logic to these gains is not always obvious. It is rare that anybody stands up and says, "This change threatens my sense of security and my position of power within the company; therefore I am against it." It is more common for individuals to act from a hidden agenda, trying to manipulate their surroundings into doing their bidding. In many cases, the gains are completely or partially unconscious for the individual in question. Actions that seemingly run counter to a person's own interests can turn out to be completely logical if you examine the unconscious forces behind them.

Within an organization, one might find some typical motives for individuals not paying attention to what is happening:

Avoidance of responsibility. If you see and recognize the negative consequences of something, you also have a responsibility to do something about it, either on your own, or by seeing to it that somebody else becomes aware of what needs to be done. By making yourself blind to parts of reality, you can always claim that you didn't know. The causes of this avoidance of responsibility range from sheer laziness to a deeply rooted psychological fear of being hit by feelings of guilt over your own shortcomings. Regardless of the cause, the effect will be the same: an organization in which the members do not take responsibility to implement change;

Fear of conflict. If you start to examine closely the events around you, you will surely notice things in others that you react to. Since this creates a risk of conflict, you may choose not to become aware of other people's behaviors. That is, you choose to make invisible, or to diminish, conflicts that simmer under the surface in order to avoid bringing them to light;

Avoiding uncertainty. Much of what takes place within an organization is contradictory, diffuse, or incomprehensible;

thus it is hard to do anything about it. Your need to feel as if you are in control may cause you to avoid seeing things that imbue you with a sense of uncertainty;

Unwillingness to violate unspoken social norms. In many organizations, people avoid doing and saying things they believe might make others uncomfortable, even if it would benefit business to do so. In order not to create internal conflicts you may, in this setting, choose, consciously or unconsciously, not to take note of what you believe others do not want people to see;

Implicit agreements. "Conspiracies of leniency" are common. If I do not see or bring up your failings, you will close your eyes to mine.

In conclusion, we could say that, in certain situations, managers and employees prioritize their own need for power, control, security, and well- being over the company's need for efficiency. For the most part, this is completely unconscious behavior. The most important inner compass for the majority of people is the diffuse gut feeling of ease or unease. We do what we can to avoid feeling bothered, insecure, or unaccepted in our environment. The gut feeling often sends stronger signals than the intellect, especially in situations that carry with them a high degree of uncertainty.

Instead of regarding the gut feeling as an important source of information, it is often dismissed as something that gets in the way of the thought process.

This does not mean that the influence of your gut feelings on what is happening is decreased, but rather the contrary: If we avoid bringing the emotional aspects to light, the risk is that they will garner way too much influence at the expense of reason.

Company X was a fairly typical company in the ways detailed here. Over the years, it had developed a corporate culture that involved employees avoiding giving feedback to, and making demands of, colleagues at their same level or higher. Within the management team, this was evidenced as, among other things, accepting a low level of involvement at meetings.

Not surprisingly, the same pattern could be observed at every level of the organization. Among employees and lower management, one spoke *about* what one thought others should do, but one did not say this directly *to* them. This behavior was justified by seemingly solid arguments. Setting standards and demanding responsibility was considered a task for management. Thus, everyone with a superior—that is to say, everyone except the CEO— could delegate the making of demands upward in the organization. Any employee who criticized a colleague was considered to be out of bounds ("playing boss") and ruining the convivial atmosphere within the company. Employees tended to use phrases like "consideration," "integrity," and "unwillingness to hurt anyone" if the failure to hold others to standards came up for discussion.

The staff's widespread habit of ignoring behaviors not benefiting the business did not simply cause these behaviors to flourish freely within the organization. By redefining these defensive behaviors in positive terms, employees also legitimized their failure to take responsibility for correcting attitudes or actions that were detrimental to the company.

For their part, management was not aware that it was actually condoning a stance that contributed to inefficiency. Nor did it understand that it had hamstrung itself when it came to dealing with the inefficiency. The demands made on subordinates were mild, bordering on ineffectual. Subordinates, in turn, very rarely made demands of one another, or of their superiors when these were present. Instead, they complained to each other behind closed doors, or in other informal situations where their complaints could in no way lead to any productive change. Grumbling in the break room came to replace direct feedback as a way of venting dissatisfactions.

The aim for the developmental process

The overall conclusion drawn by the consultants after the interviews was that the issues the management team was facing were not due to lack of understanding or lack of will among its members. Rather, the problem was *a lack of attention to the hidden interplay within the group and the organization at large*, combined with *a lack of ability to transform good intentions into efficient actions*. The lack of attention was evident both when it came to an individual's own actions and those of other people.

The interviews revealed that the members of the management team actually had a pretty good idea of what was wrong and what they themselves were doing to compound the situation. However, together, they consistently avoided focusing on it, exploring it, and reflecting on it. This avoidance took place, in part, unconsciously; in part, as a consequence of not being considered important; and in part as a way of avoiding controversy. Instead of giving meaningful feedback, employees held up guiding principles such as *factuality* and *goal orientation*, while turning a blind eye to the hidden games that often both distorted the factual issues and influenced the outcomes. The difficulty in making the leap from insight to action robbed everyone concerned of the very tools they needed to make demands and hold each other responsible.

The consultants' goal for their work with the management team became, according to the perspective garnered in the interviews:

- to increase awareness of what was actually going on in the interplay between them;
- to contribute to vitalizing the system for feedback and communication in general;
- to increase focus on actions and their consequences for the achievement of company goals; and

- to contribute to developing a deeper understanding of the problems that the group was struggling with and the ways in which they themselves were making them worse.

The point of the initial three-day meeting of the team and consultants was to create a space for the group dynamics to become visible, and for members of the group to take responsibility for them. In the daily work of the management team, the underlying dynamics were obscured by discussions about factual issues and business planning. For that reason, it made sense to take those topics off the agenda in order to increase awareness of the psychological interplay and reveal what the participants were doing in relation to each other. This does not mean that the factual issues would be considered unimportant, but, simply, that they were not the focus at this point in time. The methodology used during the three days of group development should be seen in light of this purpose.

Instead of presenting an analysis of the group from their outside perspective, the consultants strove to create a genuine learning situation together with the management team, in which insights could continuously be put into productive action. The analysis based on the initial interviews was merely a point of departure, built on a limited understanding of the situation. It was the consultants' belief that further and more in-depth insight into the issues would develop during the course of the journey. Since change is something taking place in the present moment, they assumed that the necessary information about what was wisest to do would arise continually throughout the process. Their plan of action included two additional meetings, which would focus more directly on the actions performed by the members of the team, both in the course of their work as a team and in their roles as leaders of their own departments. In this way, they believed, the gap between word and action would disappear, and the insights that were gained would benefit the business.

CHAPTER 3.
EMBRACING COMPLEXITY

The management team has completed the first half-day of their team-building event. The discussion about how to approach the team development task, and about the true meaning of "feedback," drags on and finally ceases completely. Now, the team is making tentative efforts to address the problematic and dysfunctional characteristics of Company X.

Some of the members are attempting to raise issues of importance to themselves as leaders of their departments. Robert has a problem with one of his direct reports, who reflexively questions everything he is asked to do. Jay has recent hires in the IT department who have brought some bad habits from their former consulting firms. John talks about a guy in the marketing department who is incapable of closing a deal without making promises that cause problems for those whose task it is to deliver the services down the line. In each case, the other team members listen and respond politely, but not with enough commitment to keep the discussion alive. In the absence of any useful response, the topics raised become more and more trivial, with the team members touching upon many issues without really attempting to solve them—as if they're just trying to keep the conversation going. The entire situation appears, to the consultants, as a bicycle race in which the competitors take turns in the lead but no one makes any real effort to gain speed. Mary has made several attempts to direct the conversation toward how they are acting as a team, but she has been rejected or ignored every time. Now, she is keeping a low profile, despite her growing frustration.

John is also frustrated over what he refers to as "much talk, little action," but he, too, chooses to keep a low profile, to avoid becoming the target of negative feedback from anyone who might get the idea to take that particular task seriously. Instead, he makes half-hearted attempts to engage in a discussion about whether the company's financial system is easy to manage or not. Victor, the CFO, and Jane, the administrative manager, are the only ones who have anything to say on that matter. The others contribute by offering occasional remarks without showing any signs of real enthusiasm.

One of the consultants asks, "How important is this issue of the financial system to you right now?" The answer, from Robert, the production manager, comes with lightning rapidity: "Of course it's important, and far better than not talking about anything at all." Susan agrees: "We have to find out how to make the administrative routines feasible." John gives the consultant a fierce look and says: "It's an important issue for Jane and Victor, since it will make their ability to cooperate smoother and easier. If that doesn't work out, we'll all be in big trouble." The others keep quiet. Mary looks as if she's about to make a comment, but stops herself. Richard, the CEO, looks a bit uncomfortable, clears his throat, and starts speechifying about the importance of the financial system for the survival of the company. He looks challengingly at the others in an attempt to take the team back to the discussion at hand, but Victor and Jane are now reluctant to proceed. John rivets his eyes on the consultant, who asked how important the issue of the financial system was, and says angrily, "Here you go again, telling us that what we're doing isn't good enough. Why don't you tell us what to do instead?" When the consultant answers, "How would you describe what you're doing right now?" John pointedly turns away, ignoring the consultant's question.

∗

At a cursory glance, the conversation the team was having before the consultant's question about the financial system was quite undramatic. It was about an issue that was important to all team members, even if it was fairly uncontroversial. It had also been conducted in a friendly, accepting, and matter-of-fact manner. A casual observer would probably perceive them as a team constructively discussing an important organizational issue.

At the same time, however, this discussion clearly illustrates the defensive attitude that is one of the key elements in the team's ongoing inadequate performance. By keeping such a harmless discussion going, they were actually avoiding other issues that were more important for their functioning as a team that might have been unpleasant to deal with. This is a tactic they used in their regular meetings as well. This defensive quality becomes obvious when the consultant asks about the importance of the topic being discussed. His fairly inoffensive question is perceived as a statement and, moreover, as an attack that has to be fended off. Instead of taking this opportunity to reflect on their ongoing process, the group rallies together in defense of their behavior.

Richard's stressing the importance of the financial system is another indication of the team's defensive stance. Statements that are so self-evident and lacking in substance that no one can raise any objection to them are common symptoms of teams who are avoiding dealing with unpleasant core issues.

Thus, the financial system discussion can be regarded as a manifestation of the team's reluctance to address controversial issues. The consultants, watching the course of events from outside the group, have no difficulty seeing through the defensive maneuvers being used by the team to maintain equilibrium. Their challenge is to make the team members aware of these maneuvers, and to help them understand the impact of these on the team's performance.

Moreover, every attempt by the consultants to describe how the team members are dealing with team issues, as well as with one another, have resulted in nothing but further defensive reactions. Despite that, the consultants persist in doing precisely what the team members themselves are avoiding doing: verbally expressing how they are perceiving the team's attempts to cope with the situation. The consultants do this for two reasons. First, it gives support to those in the team who sense what is going on and want to change it, although they do not dare to assert themselves in the current group climate. Second, the consultants regard the team's increased level of defensiveness as an *asset*, not an obstacle.

The logic behind this attitude toward resistance is not obvious. Shouldn't the consultants do whatever it takes to *reduce* the defensiveness? This question points to the very essence of change, and we'll come back to it later in this book. At this point, it is sufficient to establish that the consultants consider it necessary for the defensiveness to grow even more evident, in order to make it impossible for the team members not to become aware of it, and, further, not to deal with it.

The alternative would have been to suggest some activity that might relieve the team's frustration, or to help them to look for "positive" solutions, instead of focusing on the problems. Either of these alternatives would probably have been greeted with applause, but by choosing them, the consultants would actually have become accomplices in the subconscious strategy the team is using to ignore—and thereby maintain—its difficulties, namely, to bypass them in the guise of doing something positive.

If the team members had been less reluctant to look at themselves, they might have been able to discover some of the defensive strategies that impaired their performance. Two such strategies are clearly shown in the example above: He Who Sees the Problem Becomes the Problem; and Apparent Matter-of-Factness. Let's look at both.

He who sees the problem becomes the problem

As we have seen, when someone, in this case the consultant, calls attention to something the team is avoiding, he or she becomes the target of more or less aggressive attacks from the others. It is as if the problem comes into existence when it is pointed to, and is caused by the person who points to it. Instead of dealing with the message, the team members shoot the messenger. This not only happens when the team perceives an attack from outside; it is also part of a type of "corrective system" that strikes all of the team members whenever they do "stick their necks out." So far, Mary has been the main target for this corrective pressure, but no team member has been left unaffected. It fosters an atmosphere of cautiousness, and a feeling that one needs rock-solid arguments to say anything that may be seen as controversial. That, combined with the impossibility of predicting what might actually be viewed as controversial, causes the team members to stay on safe ground. The unfortunate consequence of this is that the team is deprived of vital information from its members, as well as being deprived of their unbridled energy and creativity.

On a deeper, unconscious level, this is a kind of buck-passing game regarding the question, "Who's to blame?" It is risky to expose weakness in a group climate where the level of trust is low, because the one who does so runs the risk of being used as a scapegoat for the shortcomings of the whole team.

This is not merely fantasy. Most of the team members reported having had the experience of being used this way when they have tried to address a concern they had. The risk is at its highest when team members are frustrated from not being able to fulfill their responsibilities as a management team. Everyone feels burdened with a sense of guilt and powerlessness, and it can be very tempting to move the weight of those negative feelings onto someone else's shoulders. While doing that provides momentary relief, however, it solves neither the problems being struggled with nor those caused by the lack of trust that exists in the first place. The latter, in fact, are, rather, aggravated, since no one can be sure that his or her weaknesses will not be exploited the next time the team is looking for a scapegoat.

Playing on feelings of guilt is a common and, usually, very effective means of manipulation. In the episode above, this is exemplified by the sudden support for Victor and Jane shown by many of the team members when the consultant interfered in the financial discussion. If these team members had genuinely cared about Jane's and Victor's problems, they would likely have expressed it by showing more interest in them before the consultant's intervention. Instead, their true purpose was to make the consultant feel like an insensitive brute who had better leave the group in peace. This kind of manipulation is not just about playing on guilty feelings and scapegoating, it undermines the foundation of trust itself when team members show support as a means to exert power.

There are many ways—both more and less subtle— that team members let fellow members know their conduct is undesired. Voicing negative comments or making faces are among the less subtle. The up-side of these expressions, though, is that they can be heard or seen, and commented on by the targeted member, even if his or her reacting to these expressions might be regarded as undesirable behavior as well.

More often, though, punishment for "bad" team behavior is carried out by ignoring the message as well as the messenger. In the context of human interaction, where social responsiveness is the very breath of life, a non-response is perceived as extremely unpleasant. It is also a more effective punishment in the sense that the subject of it is not able to pinpoint any punishing behavior on the part of the others. If he does, nevertheless, try to accuse the others of such behavior, they have only to respond unsympathetically to his complaint, and the punishment will be complete.

Of course, it isn't quite true that there is no punishing behavior to pinpoint when a team ignores one of its own members. It is a common misunderstanding that there is such a thing as neutral behavior in human interactions. Most of us try to keep a neutral expression during meetings, convinced that in doing so we promote a matter-of-fact atmosphere that is beneficial for the performance of the team. In reality, though, such behavior contributes to an overall lack of enthusiasm and a general feeling of discouragement, which often denies responsibility for itself with terms like "we have a way of doing things around here." This is a common expression for team members who make themselves blind to the real impact they have on one another. We will discuss this particular kind of blindness—known as "skilled incompetence"—in chapter 5.

Apparent matter-of-factness

The arguments for the importance of the financial-system discussion in the example above are seemingly characterized by matter-of-factness and consideration. This obscures the fact that neither the discussion itself, nor the arguments for having it, were based on a close analysis of what was needed to accomplish the team's task at hand. Indeed, what the team did was mainly satisfy their emotional needs. Team members felt a deep frustration due to their feelings of uncertainty and powerlessness, even if some of them were better at concealing that than others. However, no one was willing to put his or her frustration on the agenda, for that would have been risking "becoming the problem," as described above. The mixture of frustration and lack of trust caused a strong urge for security, control, and conflict-avoidance. A matter-of-fact issue—the financial system discussion—with no major disagreements served that purpose well.

However, this apparent matter-of-factness is more than just the way team members chose to deal with this particular team development event. It also played a significant role in their everyday decision-making process.

Team members, as a rule, tend to look at input from others purely as factual statements, rather than as expressions of emotional needs or attempts to gain power or advantage based on some hidden agenda. This diminishes their ability to evaluate that input, an evaluation that is necessary for unbiased decision-making.

Since team members are unable to see the emotional aspects of the input, they are, therefore, unable to address the true motivation behind it; they are prevented from challenging the input-giver's attempts to manipulate the team for his or her own egoistic purposes. This holds true for *deliberate* manipulations to obtain advantage, as well as for *unconscious* maneuvers to avoid discomfort.

A prerequisite for an efficient decision-making process is that the information used is unpolluted by biased and manipulative elements. This means that the rational as well as the emotional motivation of the person giving the information has to be scrutinized.

A paradoxical consequence of management teams focusing exclusively on factual matters is that emotional aspects will exert an unreasonably strong impact on the work process. When ignored, rather than being subjected to critical examination, emotional aspects are given free reign. In many organizations, the emotional undercurrents that exist constitute a subversive power that, left uncontrolled, will push the course of things in an unintended direction. That is one reason why many attempts at organizational change are unsuccessful, in spite of—or perhaps due to—their being rationally carried out.

The apparent matter-of-factness on the part of the management team is not just caused by their reluctance or inability to consider the emotional aspect of what is happening. It is also a consequence of the rationalistic approach that is predominant in the management team, and in Company X as a whole. According to this approach, reality can be understood in terms of cause and effect, i.e., by applying linear logic. Since our inclination for linear thinking is a frequent cause of deadlocks and obstacles to change, we shall next take a closer look at that phenomenon.

Linear versus non-linear logic

Linear cause-and-effect chains are ubiquitous in our everyday life. If I press the start button on my computer (cause), I hear a familiar "ting-a-ling," the screen lights up, and the usual icons appear (effect). If I kick a pebble on the sidewalk with a definite impact, it will roll a certain distance, depending on weight, shape, friction, etc. I can roughly predict where it will end up. If I have adequate measurement instruments at hand and apply the laws of physics, I can make this prediction with fairly good precision.

Suppose, now, that I perform a kick with exactly the same physical impact, but this time I target a dog on the sidewalk. The sequence of cause and effect in this case is much less obvious, since it must be understood in the context of an encounter between two living beings: An unfamiliar dog might sink his teeth into my calf, while my own faithful companion would whimper and give me an injured glance. Furthermore, if I directed a similar kick at a human being, the entire matter would take on a social context. He would estimate the intention behind it, and his personality and previous experiences would also influence his response to such a violation. The effect of my kicking him would be the outcome of a complex interpretation process. Afterward, I could make an educated guess as to why he gave me a punch in the nose instead of calling the police or running away, but I could not have made a solid prediction. In short, my attempt to find a linear cause-and-effect chain will get lost in the immense *complexity* that characterizes the situation.

Other causal relations are *circular*, *i.e.*, the different parts of the system are mutually influencing one another. In long-term relationships between people, this is the norm; linear cause-and-effect chains are exceptions. The wife withdraws to escape her husband's nagging. The husband nags because his wife withdraws from him. Each sees the other's actions as the cause of his or her behavior. Attempts to solve the problem are based on linear logic from both parties: "If you only would act differently...." Since both are trying to break off a circular connection by using linear logic, the problem continues to exist.[5]

An organization can be looked upon as a vast web of circular interpersonal relations. Every action gives rise to reactions, which cause new actions, giving rise to further reactions—and so on, endlessly. Generally, these chains of influence are quite trivial. A man comes to the office in a bad temper. In the elevator, he snaps at a colleague, who gets annoyed. When the colleague reaches his desk, now in a bad mood, a clerk at the desk next to his takes his grim face as a sign of displeasure with something that he, the clerk, has done. Instead of checking out whether his presumption is correct, he is curt toward another colleague while asking for information. This colleague . . . and so on. The bad temper that triggered this chain of reactions might have been caused by a matrimonial

---

[5] For a further discussion of these deadlocks and how to unlock them, see Watzlawick, P., *et al.*, *ante*.

quarrel, or by something that happened at work the day before. In most cases, it is futile to try to find the root cause of the inappropriate pattern of interaction, since every action can be regarded as a reaction to something that someone else did before.

What can be done, though, is to focus immediately on negative reactions, find out what is behind them, and, most important, keep an open mind for the possibility that we ourselves have contributed to them. Instead of doing that, though, we often give ourselves a linear explanation, making ourselves victims of the bad behavior of others. Since our colleagues might be doing the same, we create vicious circles of misbehavior, misinterpretations, and mistrust. This is one of the main reasons why workplace conflicts can last for years, stubbornly resisting every attempt to solve them.

Why is it that we are so inclined toward linear thinking, and so disinclined toward grasping non-linear causal connections? A probable reason might be that early in life we learned to pay attention to cause-and-effect connections, in order to avoid unpleasant consequences of mistakes and dangerous actions.

In addition, it is obviously joyful to cause effects in the world. An infant can squeeze a horn over and over again, gleeful each time at producing that sound.

The concept that the world can be linearly understood is reinforced in schools, and especially in higher education, where a right answer exists for every question, and the ability to detect cause-and-effect connections is rewarded with good grades. Furthermore, the striving for objectivity and measurability causes an inclination, in both teachers and students, toward knowledge that can be expressed in terms of cause and effect.

As psychologist Donald T. Campbell points out, we have a hereditary biological tendency to prefer tangible aspects of reality to abstract ones:

> "The natural knowledge processes with which we are biologically endowed somehow make objects like stones and teacups much more 'real' than social groups or neutrinos, so that we are offended of (sic) the use of the same term 'real' to cover both instances . . . ."[6]

An epistemological explanation pointing in the same direction is that Western culture since Aristotle has cultivated causal thinking as the principal way to understand the world. We find that perspective in its purest form within the Positivistic school of philosophy, developed during the Age of Enlightenment in the eighteenth century. According to this theory of science, a theoretical assumption is expressed in a hypothesis that can be verified or rejected by means of empirical research or investigation. This approach gave rise to an objective and verifiable body of knowledge, in contrast to the religious and mystical conceptions characterizing previous

---

[6] Campbell, D., "Common Fate, Similarity, and Other Indices of the Status of Aggregates of Persons and Social Entities," *Behavioral Science,* 3 (1958), p. 17.

epochs. In addition to that, it has played an enormously important role in the process of building prosperity in Western civilization.

In everyday life, our predilection for linear thinking probably springs from a wish for predictability, orderliness, and control in our daily activities. The alternative, *i.e.*, the feeling of groping in a complex, evasive, and only partially comprehensible reality, is far more dissatisfying. Furthermore, linear thinking provides our brains with an economical way in which to deal with information. If we can boil down a complex phenomenon to a single factor—in this case a root cause—we can disregard all the other elements involved, and, thus, free up our brains to handle other tasks. For example, knowing the linear chain that exists between putting a letter into the mailbox and having it delivered to the addressee saves us the trouble of worrying about what is happening to it at each step along the way. In doing so, it liberates our brain's capacity to focus on other problems we must solve, or to do something else that would be more fun.

The negative consequences of linear logic arise when we apply it to connections that are non-linear, *i.e.*, when the causal links are circular or too complex to be described in cause-and-effect terms. In these types of cases, the immediate feeling of mastering reality turns out, in the long run, to be an illusion. The problem that was supposed to be solved reappears, sometimes in a new guise. Sticking to a linear strategy leads only to the endless treatment of new symptoms, as it never permits us to grasp the underlying dynamic that generates these symptoms.

Our culture's scientific understanding of non-linear aspects of physical and social reality is a comparatively recent phenomenon. In the 1950's, general systems theory was developed to describe how reciprocally dependent elements influence one another, as well as the system within which they exist as a whole. A decade later, chaos theory added to this understanding the complexity of *iterative* systems, *i.e.,* systems in which an output is fed back into the system to generate a new output…and so on, continuously. Population growth models are examples of iterative systems, where the outcome one year is used as input the next. The chain of events starting with the man snapping at his colleague, described earlier, is another example. The outcomes of each subsequent encounter between the office employees served as input, influencing the subsequent course of events in the interpersonal system of the workplace. This iterative quality of systems built on human interactions makes chaos theory highly relevant for a deeper understanding of organizational life.

The term *chaos* in this context is not to be confused with haphazardness or total lack of order. Rather, it denotes phenomena with such a high degree of complexity that they cannot be predicted with any reasonable precision. The expression "extreme sensitivity to initial conditions," commonly known as the "butterfly effect," is an example of unpredictability due to system complexity:

A butterfly performing an extra wing-flap in the Amazon jungle can determine whether or not a tornado will arise over the Pacific Ocean three weeks later. The dramatic and unpredictable impact of such an infinitesimal event on the global climate system makes it impossible to make accurate weather forecasts more than a couple of weeks ahead, no matter how much technology is employed.

General systems theory, as well as chaos theory, distinguishes between *stable* and *unstable* systems. A stable system gravitates toward a state of equilibrium. A pendulum has its state of equilibrium in a vertical position, and every swing takes it closer to this point, unless an external force is exerted upon it. Unstable systems can be exemplified by a modern fighter aircraft—for example, the F-22 Raptor. To make it possible for the craft to keep a steady course, rather than, say, fluttering like a moth or floating down like an autumn leaf, the steering system has to make continuous adjustments, which will compensate for the fundamental instability of the craft. The reason for equipping a plane with such a degree of instability is to facilitate its ability to carry out evasive maneuvers—such as dodging missiles or chasing enemy planes— without having to battle against a strong tendency to keep going in a straight line. Stable systems, on the other hand, can be exemplified by old-time fighter planes, such as the F-14 Tomcat. Even if the pilot loses consciousness or all the steering systems collapse, it will continue to move straight ahead until a lack of fuel causes it to fall into the gravitation pull.

Many systems, especially the iterative ones, in which the output is fed back into the system, can oscillate between stable and unstable states. The "butterfly effect" (*i.e.*, the extreme sensitivity to initial conditions mentioned above) implies that the system is unstable. If, on the other hand, the system is in a state of stability, the opposite prevails; it regains its state of equilibrium, irrespective of the input.[7] This peculiar difference between unstable and stable systems, regarding their response to input, has consequences for how change can be implemented in complex systems, *i.e.*, in organizations, groups, or even individuals.

To manage organizational change successfully, one has to learn to differentiate the non-linear logic of human perception, motivation, and interaction from the linear logic of systems for production, economy, and information. If the non-linear human aspects are addressed with a linear approach, they will indeed be easier to handle, but there will also be a substantial risk that the measures taken will lead to mock solutions with no impact on the real issues. The prevailing way in which leadership-training programs are designed, following traditional educational models, is quite compatible with the linear way of thinking, with which people in most organizations are comfortable. Nevertheless, imparting more knowledge does not help much if the real problem is that the receivers of that knowledge do not use what they already

---

[7] For a closer exposition of the dynamics of iterative systems, see Gleick, J., *Chaos; Making a New Science* (London: Abacus, 1988), chapters 1 and 6.

know. The hope that such an approach will work is a manifestation of a type of mental deadlock, which is known in change theory as "more-of-the-same" or "when-the-solution-becomes-the-problem."[8] Repeating the same solution over and over again leads only to a strengthening of the mindset from which the problem originally arose. That is, the more you try to change, the more you get stuck in the same old rut. The consequence of this is a kind of "vaccination" against real change. By giving an ineffectual dosage of input from managers and management consultants, you only mobilize the kind of mental immune defense that is usually named "change resistance."

Thus, general systems theory will complicate the organizational picture, but the consequences of chaos theory for the possibility of organizational change appears to be downright discouraging. Either the system is stable and will revert to its original condition no matter what measures are taken, or it is unstable and, therefore, impossible to direct, since the effect of infinitesimal input can be immense in an unpredictable way.

Fortunately, reality is not quite so dramatic. An organization is an intricate amalgamation of stabilizing and destabilizing elements. In addition to solid organizational structures and systems, the human need for security is a potent stabilizer. On the other hand, the prevailing order is constantly challenged by the unpredictability of the surrounding world. The merit of chaos theory is that it

---

[8] Watzlawick, P., *et al., ante,* chapter 3.

pinpoints some interesting and highly relevant aspects to consider when leading and changing organizations.

It seems reasonable to draw at least three conclusions from chaos theory:

You cannot lead a complex organization by remote control in a changing world. In this context, "leading by remote control" refers to management by directions, rules, and frameworks, and also by visions, plans, and objectives. These methods have in common that they can be compared to throwing a message in a bottle into the ocean and hoping it will be found by the desired recipient. Many managers send their directives down the levels of the organization hoping they will have the desired impact on subordinates. The follow-ups are usually conducted by formalized reports, which inevitably leads to watered-down and outdated information.

An alternative, considering the non-linear nature of a complex organization, would be to evolve a corporate culture where everybody takes responsibility for doing the thousands of small, everyday adjustments needed to deal with the changing demands of the surrounding world. That would imply enhanced attention to the here-and-now course of events, so that they can be addressed and corrected immediately. The most important instrument for managing such a culture is continuous feedback, directing the thousands of daily actions toward company goals.

Every organization should find the optimal level of instability they need to be able to match the changes in the surrounding world. This implies, to recycle the airplane metaphor used above, becoming a little less like the F-14 Tomcat and a little more like the F-22 Raptor. The wish for harmony, comfort, and security is legitimate, but there is a risk that these values would be given priority to the ability to make swift changes of course. I recommend "creative instability," which is characterized by profound sincerity, clarity, and mutual accountability, even if that raises the level of conflict. The vitalization caused by such an approach would probably increase business efficiency as well as quality of life for all employees.

To change the corporate culture, you have to destabilize it. Since a stable system has an excellent capacity for foiling attempts to change it, destabilization is a prerequisite for true organizational change. Consequently, too strong a need for controlling the change process can jeopardize the desired outcome. Many necessary transformations have been delayed or gone unrealized because of the unwillingness or/and incapability of anxious leaders to allow the temporary disorder that signifies the transition from obsolete to up-to-date.

A fourth conclusion, emanating from the other three, is: *The competence to exert influence on non-linear systems differs from the ability to manage cause-and-effect chains*. Awareness of the deeper levels of interpersonal processes, and the courage to intervene within them, is more important than the ability to make analyses.

This does not mean that an intellectual understanding of change dynamics is unimportant. Obviously, the inability of Company X's management team members to grasp their shared reality is not only due to their avoiding emotional discomfort; their cognitive map is also inadequate. They stick to a linear and mechanical way of thinking, rooted in times when the pace of change was slower and plain directives were sufficient for managing the company. This does not mean they are ignorant of modern leadership and management philosophy, but that knowledge has little impact on their actual behavior. The team members have all taken several courses on leadership, but those have actually made the knowing-doing gap worse, as team members have not implemented their acquired insights in the workplace, nor have they confronted the ingrained attitudes in Company X. The linear pedagogical thought behind such courses is that insight leads to action. However, the evidence for this causal chain, no matter how plausible it seems to be, is poor. It is easy to find people in almost every organization who know a lot about what should be done but do little or nothing about it. In my experience, the statement that action leads to insight is as valid as the reverse, if not more so.[9]

The development process that Company X's management team is undergoing is designed to give them an

---

[9] This phenomenon, i.e., when insights, decisions, plans, etc., substitute for action, is brilliantly described in: Pfeffer, J. and Sutton, R.I., *The Knowing-Doing Gap* (Cambridge, MA.: Harvard Business School Press, 1999).

opportunity to experience ways of handling matters that differ greatly from their habitual ones. The logic behind this can be described by the following sequence: increase attention to and awareness of what is really happening; foster the courage to bring what has been attended to into the light; make the members accountable for the consequences of what they do, or fail to do, based on the insights gained; and finally, build a cooperative culture that recognizes openness, the ability to take action, and reciprocal accountability.

Once again, silence has fallen on the team. Some of the members seem to be mentally searching for a topic important enough to discuss, while others look defiantly uninterested. Finally, Jay, the CIO, breaks the silence, saying, "I'm thinking about what happened in our last team meeting." All eyes turn to him, and he continues. "I mean, when we talked about how to organize the IT support for our new line of production." He looks around to see if anyone is willing to join in the discussion. Encouraged by signs of interest in the eyes of the others, he says, "We agreed that my guys should look at solutions, and then discuss them with your people." He looks at John, Mary, and Robert. "But then it turned out that you were already working

LARS J CLEMEDSON   75

on your own solutions, so everyone was fighting for their own ideas instead of working with us. I tried to address that issue last time, but I didn't feel I got anywhere."

Robert is the first to respond: "My people are used to running the production their own way, so I think they just went ahead as they're used to doing when new products are on the way. Besides, they don't think that your guys understand our reality. We need tangible solutions that everyone can easily catch onto. No one has the time to look in manuals, or to run off to ask somebody else when the system is screwing up."

Jay answers by giving a wordy explanation of the advantages of having an integrated system throughout the company. The burst of vitality that had, at first, resulted from his initiation of an interesting topic is now flattening out, and the team falls back into its previous languid state. Now it is Jay, John, and Robert who get entangled in technical, matter-of-fact issues, while the others do their best to look interested.

*

As Jay makes an effort to address an issue that is of great concern to him, he points to at least two core problems at Company X: (1) *decisions are realized only partially, or not at all,* and (2) *there is insufficient co-operation between departments.* The latter is due to widespread incapacity — especially on the part of department heads — to prioritize the needs of the company-as-a-whole over short-term benefits to their own, individual fields of responsibility. The meeting he has referred to as "our last team meeting" was the management team's first opportunity to follow-up on a decision made a couple of months earlier. According to that decision, the role of the IT department was to change significantly. Until then, the IT department had been serving as an internal consulting agency, vending its services to the rest of the company. Now, it was to take on the role of strategic coordinators who would tell the other departments what to do. This move was intended to take IT from an obscure and peripheral position to the very core center of the company's exercise of power.

Most of the team members had been content after reaching this decision, for it meant that, for once, they had been able to come to an agreement in a matter of great strategic importance. Jay had been particularly satisfied, since he had expected his power in the company would be strengthened as a result of the change. John and Robert, on the other hand, were less pleased with the new order. They had come up with a lot of arguments against giving the IT department such overall responsibility and power. They had been quite content to use the department as helpers when they called IT in, and they wanted it to stay that way. After raising several objections to giving

IT so much power, however, they had to give up when Richard, the CEO, gave his unreserved support to the proposed organizational change. The meeting had concluded with the consensus that the new order should be implemented promptly.

When Robert met with his own team of managers, after this meeting of the top management team, he acted as the loyal retainer he had become after more than 25 years in the company. He described the decision objectively and stressed the fact that it had been unanimous. Moreover, he described the arguments raised against it, but also the counter-arguments that had, in the end, made the balance tilt in favor of the decision. No one could, at least not at a quick glance, assert that he did not pass this information on to his department in a responsible and conscientious way.

Yet, quite a different story emerges upon closer scrutiny. Robert's dutiful reporting, without enthusiasm, and with bodily and facial expressions hinting, "I don't like this," sent a signal that his co-workers had no problem deciphering, after having had Robert as their boss for many years. It said, "We can't change this, so let's see if we can get around it some way." In order to secure support from the others in undermining the decision, he spent considerable time describing the problems it would cause to production. When he concluded, "Let's give the IT guys a chance," no one believed him. Instead, the meeting resulted in increased efforts by his management team to make their own systems immune to intrusion from the IT department. One way of doing this was to intensify their contacts with the external suppliers they had been using right along, instead of cutting them off and letting Jay's IT department take over. At the same time, as a cover-up, they had perfunctory meetings with representatives of the in-house experts from Jay's department.

Jay knew nothing about the schemes of Robert's team, but he did notice the consequences of them. Intuitively, he sensed foul play, and by addressing the issue at this point, he hoped to bring Robert's actions to light. John's marketing people reacted in a way similar to those in Robert's production department, but they took the initiative to discuss their objections openly with Jay and his people, instead of secretly undermining the IT department's new authority. In Mary's customer relations department, the decision was mainly accepted, except for some complaints about a wiseacre attitude on the part of the IT experts.

Jay's directing his feedback to the three of them, in spite of the apparent differences in the gravity of their obstruction, was a way for him to avoid an open clash with Robert. By diluting the direct feedback addressed to him, Jay also made it easier for all the team members to steer the focus away from the controversial essence of his comment, and to find a less delicate line of discussion. Their reviving the discussion that had preceded the reorganization of the IT department served no real purpose, since no one called for the decision to be cancelled. It was just a convenient way to fend off the discomfort that dealing with the essence of Jay's feedback might have caused.

As a matter of fact, Jay could have included Mark, the purchasing manager, in the target group of his criticism. There had been some obstruction in the purchasing department as well, but Mark's skill at giving the impression of cooperation was better developed than that of the others. He had approached Jay, admitting, in a regretful voice, that they had been unable to get the staff to adapt the new IT strategy, and assuring him that this was a "start-up" problem that would soon be taken care of. He also directed Jay's attention to Robert, John, and Mary's deceitful way of evading the management team's decision. Jay had allowed himself to be taken in, and did not see through Mark's manipulations.

Robert's attempt to circumvent the management team's decision, as well as Jay's addressing that same issue without directly confronting Robert, are two examples of *defensive routines* in organizations. Since this phenomenon plays a crucial part in our understanding of the problems that the team is struggling with, we'll take a closer look at it in chapter 5. At this point, we'll simply establish that Jay's commendable initiative was effectually smothered by defensiveness, to which he himself also contributed.

Thus, there was a considerable risk that the episode would add to the spirit of dejection that characterized the team. To counteract that, the consultants intervened to encourage Jay to be more direct in his feedback. This helped him put his concerns into words, although he still did not dare to criticize Robert. Instead, he chose to reveal how disappointed he was about the others begrudging him his advancement. Everyone could see that it also made him sad, even if he pretended to look as indifferent as he could.

Jay's sincere attempt to describe how he felt thawed the frosty climate that surrounded the team. After a while, they were all engaged in a lively discussion of what responsibility they each took in processing and implementing decisions. Though the exchange of views was kept on a level where no one's shortcomings were singled out, nevertheless, it was characterized by a genuine wish on the part of the team members to understand how they impaired their own teamwork, and how they could improve. Most of them recognized themselves in Jay's description; all of them had had the experience of seeing something of great importance to themselves succumb to other team members' reluctance to implement it in their own departments. They were, also, all beginning to realize that they frequently, and almost reflexively, went against suggestions from other team members, regardless of the effect it had on their ability to reach a mutual decision.

Still, however, there were attempts to find simplistic solutions. Jane suggested that they try to agree on regulations pertaining to how to implement and follow-up management team decisions. This suggestion was turned down, with the counter-argument that they had already devoted several meetings to working out such regulations and these had not lasted for more than a couple of months in the past. Robert wanted Richard to take a firmer stand on team discussions, but that proposal failed to arouse any enthusiasm among the rest of the team. Faint attempts to blame the team's shortcomings on circumstances beyond their control were also made and disregarded. There was always someone who brought the team back to the core issue: their own collaborative process.

Thus, we can see that the team's way of approaching the task has changed significantly. Their increased engagement following Jay's open-hearted contribution indicates an awakening willingness to scrutinize how they relate to one another and work together. Their dropping the most controversial part of what Jay expressed is mainly due to their uncertainty about where it would end if they penetrated down to the bottom of the matter. This ambivalent attitude toward exploring their shared reality is typical for teams of all kinds, not only managerial ones. Each member's wish to generate the efficiency they all strive for is counter-balanced by the fear that their own contribution to the inefficiency might be brought to light. Furthermore, as we have seen, the members receive some advantages from the present team culture, even if they also suffer from it. Since they want to get rid of the drawbacks without giving up the advantages, they each try to pursue their goals without revealing their true motives. This leads to guarded, cautious, and, in the end, feeble actions which are dissatisfying to all of them. At the same time, that dissatisfaction is a strong driving force toward change. By not doing anything to mitigate dissatisfaction, the consultants are expecting it to propel a genuine motivation for behavioral change.

Another promising sign is the increasing tendency on the part of the members to become more open and personal in describing their thoughts and feelings about the situation. Jane said she now and then left the management team meetings with a vague feeling of discomfort, and that the feeling could last as long as a couple of days. Robert and Mary talked about how nice it would be if there had been more solidarity within the team. Robert, who had been a basketball coach in his spare time before he became swamped with work, spoke about the sense of community he had experienced working with the members of that team, and everyone could see how he longed for a chance to experience that feeling again. John said he found the sluggishness of the management team discussions irksome, and he admitted that he did little to conceal that from his direct reports. He acknowledged his disloyalty in doing that, but he did not detect much loyalty from the other team members, either.

This comment, which had been vigorously contradicted just an hour before, was now met with silent nods of recognition. Even Richard tried to be more open, although that only ended up in the same old way as usual, with him lecturing them about the necessity of taking responsibility for the company as a whole. They had heard it all before, but even so, this time, instead of responding with their usual blank stares, they actually showed signs of interest, and even self-examination. When they finally broke for dinner, it was with a new spirit of affinity and dawning optimism.

CHAPTER 4.
COMMUNICATION, FEEDBACK, AND THE DECISION PROCESS

When the team comes together again after the dinner break, they are in high spirits. It takes quite a while before the jokes and laughs fade and focus is redirected to more serious matters. Then, silence is falling on them, sprung out of thoughtfulness rather than the defensiveness that was the case earlier in the day. The emotional climate has apparently changed, even if no one in the room could pinpoint exactly what brought about the difference.

After a while, John turns to Richard: "I've been thinking of what you said before dinner, that you're struggling to make us work as a team. What can we do to help you with that?" Richard looks a bit surprised at the question and, after thinking for a moment, he answers, "I'd like to see more commitment to the issues we are discussing, especially those about our future, how we are going to work together, and other matters that concern the company as a whole—and, therefore, should concern all of us."

When nobody says anything, he continues. "The discussion about outsourcing our production of printed material, for example. It ended up in a dispute between Robert and me; the rest of you said nothing. That matter is your concern as much as it is his, so everyone should have comments on it." Richard is looking at John as he says those last words, so John feels compelled to answer, "Well, I got the impression that the matter was already settled, and I had nothing to say about it, anyhow. The decision seemed okay to me."

Robert joins the conversation, pointing out that he still thinks it was a bad decision, but he has come to terms with it. He tries to reopen the "matter-of-fact" discussion again, but the consultants stop him, this time with no objections from the rest of the team.

Susan turns to Richard, asking, "Do you mean that we are more like lone wolves than a real team?" Before Richard has time to answer, one of the consultants intervenes: "Is that what you mean, Susan?" She replies in the affirmative after a moment of hesitation, and then she explains there were several occasions when her co-workers have felt discouraged trying to implement personnel policies throughout the company.

When she stops talking and no one says anything, one of the consultants picks up the conversation. "Do you feel discouraged in this team?"

"No," Susan replies, "not really—but of course it's not fun when you give a suggestion and get neither a 'yes' nor a 'no.'"

"So, as a matter of fact, you feel discouraged?" the consultant asks.

"Maybe a little, yes."

There is still no response from the others, so the consultant continues. "Is there someone in the team who makes you feel more discouraged than the others?"

Susan hesitates for a moment, before replying that she cannot point to any of them. Rather, it is the overall attitude of the team that she feels is negative to her propositions. She persists in not singling anyone out when the question is rephrased in several different ways; it is obvious that she feels uncomfortable. Instead of clarifying her message, however, she tries to recant it by saying that it's really not a big problem.

Richard intervenes with a long harangue about the importance of personnel matters, and why other issues, in spite of that, have been given priority. Soon, the others are squirming. They all hear what he is saying, but they are lost about his purpose in saying it. Neither do they seem to remember that the discussion really was about how Susan feels about how she is treated in the team.

John and Mark exchange meaningful glances during Richard's homily. One of the consultants catches that and calls attention to it. Mark says, "It's nothing," and John shows his unwillingness to put the meaning of his making faces into words by looking unsympathetic. Nobody else wants to seize the opportunity and give feedback to Richard on his patronizing verbiage, so the subject is dropped.

The silence that follows is eventually broken by John, who says, "Well, I think we've come as far as we can by discussing how we work together. Let's work out some tangible proposals on how to structure our working process from now on." He turns to the other team members, and then to the consultants, but they choose not to reply.

Jane says, unconvincingly, "Yes, perhaps we should do that." The others are silent, showing no inclination to buy into John's proposal. He looks around him with an air of frustration and resignation, but he says nothing.

At this point, we can observe a team on their way toward increased openness, plain-speaking, and directness, but they still have quite a long way to go. John wants to spotlight Richard's ambivalent attitude toward true teamwork, but he addresses the issue in an indirect and insidious way.

By doing so, he is testing whether his attempt to challenge Richard's leadership is supported by the others, since he regards it to be too risky to push that issue by himself.

Similarly, Susan expresses her opinion by asking a question instead of making a statement. When she elucidates her criticism of the way the team responds to her initiatives, she assigns blame to all the team members equally—as Jay did before the dinner break. Like him, she also backs off when she's invited to address a single team member directly.

No one really believes her when she alleges that she feels equally counteracted by all her teammates. They all know that Robert and John do whatever they can to keep the personnel department out of their affairs, and that they obstruct the department's proposals in a more or less subtle way—one of which is by ignoring Susan's input in the management team meetings, even when her suggestions have no impact on their own departments. It is only when Richard or someone else supports her that they argue against her proposals, usually with a condescending undertone.

In spite of the fact that all of them have witnessed this at several occasions, they let her, now, back out of the feedback she was about to give. Of course, it is no surprise that Robert and John do so. They have been quite successful keeping the personnel department off their backs, and they have no wish to put *that* on the agenda. If that were to happen, it might result in the team setting new decisions that would make it harder for them to bypass than the nebulous policies Susan's co-workers have come up with so far.

Why the other team members keep quiet is less obvious. Maybe they want to secure a similar liberty of action for themselves, not regarding this issue, but in matters of greater concern to them. Perhaps they intuitively ally themselves with the more powerful parties in the conflict between Susan, and Robert and John. It might also be an aspect of their skilled incapability to address a controversial issue. Maybe it is a combination of all these inducements.

A more consistent and powerful intervention from the consultants might have been to spotlight the lack of support Susan is receiving in the actual here-and-now situation being enacted now. It is obvious that the silence around her is a way to deflate her feedback. The consultant's choosing not to intervene is due to Susan's relatively low status in the team. There is a considerable risk that she, by addressing the problem, will become the problem, as we have seen this described in the previous chapter. Instead, the consultant is waiting for an opportunity when someone with higher standing will offer a similar opening to scrutinize how team members support or counteract one another in the ongoing process.

Unlike some hours ago, there is an apparent wish to deal with important and difficult issues now, but attempts to do so are still being choked by the defensive caution that has prevailed all along. Because of that, the team does not bring any of their controversial issues to conclusion, in spite of their apparent commitment to the topics raised. In the long run, this is devastating to the dawning enthusiasm that was born by the chance to be able to express what has occupied their minds for a long time.

From that perspective, John's suggestion to quit the process development and shift to more tangible issues is quite understandable. It is as if he is saying, "We've had a good experience of being able to talk to each other, but now we're heading for the same inertia as before. Let's cut before we get frustrated again." Since he is the most impatient person in the management team, he is the first to react to the towering resistance against deepening the development process.

Of course, it could be tempting for the consultants to seize upon John's suggestion. They can be pretty sure that the participants would be satisfied with their progress so far, and that they would probably be given good testimonials if they used Company X as a reference for similar work in other companies. There is a simple reason, though, for them not to yield to that temptation. By doing that, they would become part of one of the detrimental patterns reducing efficiency in this team: prioritizing their own desires—in this case the wish for a good atmosphere and being liked by the others—over organizational success. This consulting dilemma—to give them what they want, or to give them what they need—is a watershed, distinguishing consultants with professional integrity from opportunistic "quick-fixers."

Defensive qualities in the management team's communication

The core question at this point is what measures should be taken to enliven the discussions instead of allowing them to fade out. We've already indicated that one of the primary causes of the fade-out is the defensiveness and absence of openness due to insufficient levels of trust. Now, let's take a closer look at how this lack of openness and trust is manifested and reinforced by the communication between the team members.

Team communication can be defined as the link from the intention of the sender, through his or her way of expressing that intention, to the receiver's perception of the message. This far, we have seen several examples of how that link is blurred by communication deficiencies. These can be sorted into at least three areas: indistinct address; indistinct sender; and indistinct or contradictory content.

Indistinct address. In the episode above, Richard gave expression to his discontent with John's poor support when the outsourcing issue was brought up for discussion. The two of them had previously discussed the matter several times, and had generally reached agreement. At this point, Richard felt betrayed by John, but he did not tell him that directly. Indeed, he turned to John when addressing the issue, but his words were addressing the whole team. Similarly, Jay avoided confronting Robert up front regarding his obstructing the new IT strategy, as we saw in chapter 3. Susan's evasive answer to the question about who discouraged her most was another way of avoiding.

All these examples illustrate the inefficiency of the management team's internal feedback. Instead of explicitly pointing out a problem and naming an accountable person, they expressed themselves in a vague, general, and collective way. This kind of feedback can be likened to a buffet: the receiver can pick out what he or she wants to respond to, after which the sender can choose to clarify the message or not. Consequently, the message is neither obligatory for the receiver nor for the sender; they can both find a loophole to escape the situation if it becomes unpleasant.

Indirect communication like this has a crucial function in a defensive organizational culture: it makes it possible to save face, one's own as well as others'. "I let you get away with it today and you let me get away with it tomorrow." This "I scratch your back and you scratch mine" conspiracy pinions everyone when it comes to giving the feedback necessary to maintain an efficient team decision process. At the same time, however, the immediate relief from getting away without being held responsible fails to counterbalance the long-term dissatisfaction with the shallowness, inefficiency, and dejection falling upon the teamwork.

Indistinct sender. Another characteristic of team communication is that the speaker avoids standing unambiguously behind his or her words. Susan referred to "several of my co-workers," but her fellow team members had a feeling that she was talking about her own opinion. "One has to," "most people think," and "it is self-evident that" are all expressions commonly used by speakers trying to hide behind a general opinion.

Susan's behavior was also illustrative of another way to make oneself less visible as a sender: by disguising a statement as a question. In the episode above, she asked Richard if he saw them more as lone wolves than as team workers, but, as a matter of fact she was stating her own view. By using this indirect way of expression, she avoided sticking her neck out on an issue that might be controversial, especially because of Richard's alleged enthusiasm for teamwork. Wrapping a statement or a feedback in the form of a question displaces the responsibility for it from the sender to the receiver. The former can always back away from it, saying, "I just asked a question."

Still, the team members' most commonly used way of hiding their true motives was the *apparent "matter-of-factness"* discussed in chapter 3. Instead of plainly saying, "I want," or "I need," their real inducements were concealed behind a smoke screen of "It's good for the company," "our last report indicates," etc. The factual statement might be solid, but it overshadows the true motive for calling attention to just that fact at just that moment. The receiver is enticed to relate to the "matter-of-fact" content and to ignore the sender's intention for bringing it up.

A prerequisite of good communication is the sender taking responsibility for his or her message by fully and unequivocally standing behind it. Such an attitude is exquisitely shown in a key scene in the old Western movie, "Bury My Heart at Wounded Knee," in which a tribe of Native Americans have gathered to discuss how to deal with a threat to their very existence. Every man gives his opinion, and everyone ends his statement with words like: "I have spoken," or "I have said all I have to say." To me, this scene represents the archetype of firmly standing by your message and sealing it by pledging your credibility.

Indistinct or contradictory content. As shown above, ambiguity about who is sending a message, and to whom it is addressed, also obscures its content. In other instances, though, it may be the message itself that is unclear, some-times even contradictory. Several of the team members put forward their arguments in a tentative way, waiting for the reactions from the others before completing their messages. Since these reactions are seldom sufficiently affirmative, little was verbalized except this overture. He who raised the issue got the impression that the others rejected his point of view. The receivers, for their part, might have missed that the issue was brought up at all.

This can be exemplified by the discussion of the financial system mentioned in chapter 3. It started with Victor questioning how ratios were used to assist in managing the other departments and the company as a whole. His real purpose was to raise a more comprehensive and controversial issue. Today, the financial department is a service function, serving the other departments when economy expertise is required, while Victor would rather have had it transformed into a superior controlling function directly under the CEO. This would represent an upgrade for his department, similar to the one that Jay managed to get created for the IT department. This matter had been dear to Victor's heart for a long time and, in his own mind, he had brought it up on several occasions, each time only to be left feeling rejected. He was fully aware of the opposition he would have to face if he got more explicit about his intentions, since he had occasionally aired his point of view privately with the other team members. Thus, his cautious way of launching it in the management team averted that resistance, but at the cost of vaporizing his message beyond recognition. His lack of courage, combined with the insufficient level of trust in the team, restrained him from speaking his mind.

Another source of indistinctness is, paradoxically, the striving for "matter-of-factness" that marks the management teamwork in Company X. It causes all messages with emotional implications to be incomplete, since the real foundation of motivation and values is not being expressed. As mentioned before, factual statements can be used as a means to camouflage hidden motives, especially in matters involving a high degree of uncertainty, for example, anything that might have impact on the power balance of the management team. If the aim of a message is to avoid uncertainty, the reverse is often the result. The undercurrent of hidden agendas nourishes a feeling of having to be on one's guard, as well as a hesitance to counteract that feeling by putting it into words.

This kind of "matter-of-factness" in an emotionally charged discussion is a special case within a general source of indistinctness: *incongruent communication*. A message is congruent when all channels send it unanimously, *i.e.,* when verbal content is backed up by facial expression, body language, voice, etc. Incongruent messages confuse the receiver, since different parts of them point in different directions. As an example, a manager can say to one of his colleagues, "I'll support your idea one hundred percent," and, at the same time, show dislike or indifference by his voice and facial expression. A clear-sighted observer might decipher such a message in this way: "I don't think that I'll benefit most by taking this fight with you openly. Therefore, I'll pretend to support your proposal, but I'll do what I can to undermine it." Such clear-sightedness is a commodity in short supply in many organizations, especially as, if it is turned into words, it violates the unspoken rule not to upset people or cause them to lose face by challenging their hidden agendas. As a consequence, reality is concealed behind an impenetrable web of illusions treated as if they were factual. We have already discussed some of the negative consequences of that approach on team spirit: sluggishness, discouragement, and disowning responsibility.

Incongruent communication is not merely a deliberate means of manipulation. In most cases, it springs from a disinclination to disclose weakness or insecurity on the part of the sender. Most of us experience having more control of our thoughts than our feelings, and by sticking to the world of ideas, we hope not to reveal unfavorable personal qualities beyond our control. Actually, this is an illusive strategy. We expose far more of ourselves then we can hold in check. The human sensor for emotional undercurrents is a finely tuned instrument, and it is only through social training that we learn to switch it off and ignore what we see and feel. Therefore, we must regain the awareness of other people's signals that we once had in order to be able to respond to what is actually communicated.

We have already seen examples of incongruent communication in the management team of Company X. Robert's dutiful acceptance of the decision to reorganize IT support in chapter 3 is one. His lack of enthusiasm for the decision shone through, but verbally he expressed no doubts. The mixed message left it open for his direct reports to obstruct the decision, and Robert can always get away with that by referring to his words if he gets caught. Such a defensive procedure is only successful if the corporate culture comprises strong focus on "matter-of-fact" content, and a corresponding poor attention to underlying messages that are not communicated verbally.

An obvious question, after establishing the imperfection of the team's communication skills, is: Why didn't they use the three offsite days for practicing communication techniques and rhetoric? The answer is simple. All the team members have attended communication courses, in which they received solid training on how to give distinct messages to each other. That they do not use what they learned in everyday situations might seem surprising, but, on second thought, it would prove not to be so. Genuine communication has little to do with technique; rather, communications are about the courage to make ourselves vulnerable by disclosing what we think, deep down, and how we feel about what is going on, as well as about what other people say and do. Furthermore, giving a candid comment to someone in the setting of an exercise in a class differs considerably from doing that in a real-life situation. In the first case, it is done on someone else's initiative, *i.e.*, in a context that relieves the talker from the full responsibility for what is said.[10] In real life, the talker feels the opposite, that he is accountable for taking the initiative, for the content, and for how the

---

[10] In a classical experiment, social psychologist Stanley Milgram has shown that many people are prepared to do horrible things to others if told to do so by an authority. I don't think the parallel to giving tough feedback to a course-mate in a training program is far-fetched. In both cases, the threshold for hurting someone else is lowered by the possibility of disowning responsibility. See Blass, Thomas, *The Man Who Shocked the World: The Life and Legacy of Stanley Milgram* (New York: Basic Books, 2004).

message is received. The last, responsibility for how the message is received, is, perhaps, hardest to bear. Since we cannot predict how others might react to our honesty, it seems safest to keep quiet. Then, to maintain our self-esteem, we usually disguise our lack of courage behind honorable words like "consideration" and "respect."

Consequently, there are good reasons to question whether the billions that companies spend on communications trainings are well spent in terms of returns on investment. In my more than 30 years as a leadership trainer, I have never seen a person obtaining a position as a leader without being able to talk to other human beings. Obviously, the problem is to be found elsewhere.

In this case, the consultants choose to help the team members be more to the point in their communications instead of teaching them techniques. Since this is done in an actual situation in which the participants have important things to say to each other, they would expect the impact on future behavior to be much stronger than if they had conducted exercises based on fictitious cases.

Richard breaks the silence, which at this time is unpleasant to all of them. He suspects that John's attempt to change the subject is a subtle way to challenge his leadership. That, and the atmosphere of insecurity growing among the team members, urges him to take an initiative to mark his position as head of the team. If not, there is a risk that issue itself may be brought up in a way he cannot control.

Accordingly, he turns to John, saying: "Let's go back to your question about what you can do to make us a better team." That wasn't exactly what John had said, but by rephrasing it, Richard is trying to ignore the undertone of questioning his authority in John's remark, that Richard is incapable of leading the team and the company without assistance. He proceeds: "How do you evaluate your own contribution to our team spirit?" John answers, "I'm not sure that I buy this team stuff straight off. In the company where I worked before coming here, we had well-defined areas of responsibility. We reported to the CEO, and he made the decisions. It worked excellently well."

The last part of his statement isn't quite true. A conclusive reason for John leaving his old company for Company X was that he was fed up with being steamrollered by his former boss. He forgets that when he is frustrated by the lethargic decision-making process in his new management team.

Again, Richard diverts John's challenge by reviving his lecture on the superiority of teamwork to decision-making left to a single person. His audience loses interest rapidly, partially because they've heard this many times before, but mainly because they are witnessing a sham fight, where neither Richard nor John is enunciating what it is really about.

Mary is the first to respond to Richard's admonitory narrative. "I'm buying the idea of a management team, but sometimes I get the feeling that the decisions have already been made. It would be better to get all the cards on the table so we don't waste a lot of time trying to agree on an issue that's already been decided." Richard answers, apparently annoyed, that he's compelled to make more decisions by himself than he wants because the others withhold commitment and responsibility. Mary persists in saying that it isn't easy to feel committed when the real decisions are already made somewhere else. The consultants intervene, asking her to be more precise in her criticism, and also to try to see her own responsibility in the problem she is addressing. Obviously, Mary is playing the role of a victim in a situation to which she herself is contributing. After a moment's hesitation, she refers to the outsourcing discussion initiated by Richard a while ago as an example of a decision in which she did not participate. Robert, the primary stakeholder in that issue, joins by saying that he also feels disregarded. Richard answers, in a voice tinged by restrained annoyance, "Okay, I get it. I'll be better at securing your support of our decisions. Satisfied?"

The criticism directed toward Richard ceases, not because anyone believes his pledge, but, rather, because he apparently had enough of it and is prepared to use his authority to protect himself. His harsh reaction shifts focus from what had otherwise been a natural subject to explore, namely, Mary and Robert's responsibility for allowing themselves to get steamrollered by Richard. Obviously, they are delegating that responsibility upwards by putting it on him, but everyone is too disconcerted by Richard's outburst to be able to focus on anything else. Mainly for the record, the consultants call attention to the element of projection[11] in Mary and Robert's blaming Richard. Even if the mental energy is elsewhere, they would consider it detrimental to the team development process if they let it pass without comment. Then, they direct their efforts to helping team members express their reactions to Richard's behavior. Eventually, Robert says that he can understand Richard's reaction, but it makes him feel uneasy. Several of the others say they feel uncomfortable, too, and that they recognize Richard's behavior from other occasions. Jane looks as if she is about to start crying, but she is reluctant to put her feelings into words.

Richard rejects the criticism by vindicating his behavior and explaining that he had good reasons to feel attacked. The consultants interrupt him rather brusquely, telling him to listen to the feedback from the others without raising any objections. He allows himself to be stopped, and the

---

[11] The defense mechanism *projection* is explained in Appendix, p. 292.

other team members express what they think and feel without being contradicted. Finally, only Jane is left. When one of the consultants says to her, "You look unhappy," Jane starts to cry silently. Jay puts his arm around her, but the consultant asks him to return to his seat, and, turning to Jane, he asks, "Can you tell us why you're sad?" She shakes her head, saying, "It's nothing. This is me; I cry easily." The consultant decides not to drop the question, and eventually she tells about her difficulties in dealing with people who are being aggressive, especially when Richard gets angry, since she regards him as an authority. She recounts that she recognizes her reaction stems from her former marriage to an angry husband, as well as from other occasions when people have lost their tempers around her. The other team members, looking uneasy at first, still say nothing, but now their faces show warmth and sympathy. Jay, sitting next to her, takes her hand and squeezes it. Asked how she feels now, Jane answers that she's relieved she can show what a namby-pamby she is without being condemned by the others. Richard looks uncomfortable, but chooses to say nothing.

During the break that follows, Richard approaches the consultants, saying that he had expected more support from them to explain the team idea, and that he was dissatisfied with the course of events before the break. They catch a

menacing undertone, but refer calmly to the agreement, before the team development, not to spare
him when his behavior makes the shortcomings
of the team worse. He replies that, indeed, he did
agree, but he also points out several issues that hav-
en't come to the surface yet that he would prefer
they focus on.

The intensity of the group dynamics has increased considerably during the last half hour. The content of the discussion, important to them all, contributes to that, but mostly
it is caused by the "matter-of-factness" being replaced
by more emotional ways of expression. On one level,
Richard's irritation is felt as unpleasant and unwanted;
on another, deeper level, it is relieving. They have all
noticed his touchiness when he is met with opposition,
and they have discussed it among themselves, but, so far,
no one has told him what impact his behavior has on them.
Now, they seize the opportunity to give him feedback on
a behavior that has worried them for quite a long time.

The feeling of relief after Richard shows his feelings is
caused by the opening it has created, in which the others
can express their own feelings. There is a great deal of
pent-up frustration and irritation within the team, even if
most of the members are fairly good at hiding it. The current team climate, along with the fear of losing face and
exposing vulnerability, give little scope for directing the
frustration outwards, except when they talk face-to-face.
Doing that deflates the tensions, but only in a context in

which no one is obliged to take responsibility for his or her dissatisfaction by doing something to change the situation. Therefore, what is useful for short-term tension-release actually adds to long-term frustrations, which, for the most part, are directed inward. The team members' consumption of anxiolytic drugs and pills against ulcers would have been a source of general distress if they had not concealed it from each other.

Jane's showing her vulnerability and disclosing her personal shortcomings made it okay for the others to express their feelings. At first, her behavior was seen as threatening, but, gradually, a feeling of relief took over. Jay's attempting to comfort her by giving her a hug was probably based on genuine care, but it was not only that. Another motive for his stepping in might have been his own insecurity of any demands that situation might put on him if he did not stop it before that could happen. Yet another motive might have been that he projected his own vulnerability onto Jane, and he was actually comforting himself.

The consultant's preventing Jay's action might seem insensitive, but the suspicion that Jay was acting on his own behalf, rather than on Jane's, justified the intervention. An important part of the team learning process is to see through actions with hidden motives in order to prevent them from interrupting the building of openness and trust. There was no evidence that Jane's need for comfort was greater than her need for showing her feelings and being accepted for doing so. To deprive her of that opportunity, based on an assumption that she was too fragile to stand alone, would be to treat her as a helpless child and not as a competent adult.

Another reason for the consultant's intervention was that Jane's reaction was caused partly by Richard's outburst. If she had not been given an opportunity to verbalize what made her unhappy, Richard would have left the situation being looked upon as a bully, both by himself and the other team members. Not only had Jane's response curbed his motivation to continue the team development process, it had also proved to all of them that emotions are risky, and that feedback must be given with the utmost caution, if at all. Furthermore, it would have created an opening for using feelings as a means of manipulation. Everyone would have been given the possibility to ward off criticism just by showing a wounded countenance without risking having their reactions called into question.

Richard's attempt to get the consultants off his back during the break might suggest that, after all, he was feeling guilty for making Jane unhappy. Considering how the situation was resolved, this was probably more about Richard's uneasiness when encountering a woman's tears than his rejection of being depicted as a brute. However, his animosity toward the consultants can also be understood as a "prevention-is-better-than-cure" maneuver, guarding himself from getting even more unpleasant feedback in the future. Of course, the consultants could not avoid noticing the threat underlying his rebuke and, of course, that made them even more determined not to spare him when they considered his behavior detrimental to the management team's process and the company's success.

Evaluative vs. personal feedback

The course of events described above can also shed light upon some important aspects of the use of feedback. A common misconception is that feedback always amounts to one person being assessed, or even judged, by another. Certainly, this kind of *evaluative feedback* is an important tool for a superior following up the performance of a subordinate; the latter has the right to be informed of the extent to which he is fulfilling his obligations. The parties' roles are asymmetrical insofar as the distribution of power is concerned and, sometimes, also with regard to experience and knowledge relevant to the working situation. Pairs of roles like boss–subordinate, teacher–pupil, etc., are *complementary*, following an unspoken agreement that it is more reasonable for the former to evaluate the latter than the other way around.

All feedback is not evaluative, though, at least if we do not choose to use the term exclusively for assessing performance. Another option is to give *personal feedback*. This allows for one person's forthright and honest response to another person's behavior, rather than an assessment of whether that behavior is good or bad in itself; it is a means to inform a person of the impact he has on the people around him. The message behind this kind of feedback is: "What you do is important to me. It pleases or displeases me; it makes my job easier or harder; it gives me energy or it discourages me."

If that information is insufficient, the recipient of it will satisfy his need for feedback using his own imagination, which will impair his reality contact. Since these fantasies have a tendency to be negative, there is a considerable risk that they will add to suspicion and caution. Organizations with a poor feedback culture tend to be caught in the vicious circle named *paranoiagenesis*,[12] which ends in a culture of mistrust that is detrimental to the wellbeing, as well as to the performance, of the employees.

However, personal feedback is not merely important for individual satisfaction and growth. As organizations get flatter and more complex, making it more difficult to manage them with traditional methods of "command-and-control," just performing the job assignment adequately is insufficient. It becomes increasingly important that all employees, co-workers as well as managers, assume the responsibility for attuning their business activities to company goals. In addition to that, everyone must also facilitate cooperation by contributing to work motivation, creativity, and open communication. Annoying behavior cannot just be looked upon as a matter of wellbeing, it can also seriously impede productivity.

---

[12] See Erlich, H. S., "Enemies Within and Without: Paranoia and Regression in Groups and Organizations," in Gould, L.; Stapley, L.F.; and Stein, M., eds., *The Systems Psychodynamics of Organizations* (London UK: Karnac Books, 2006).

Having a corporate culture in which personal feedback is a natural part of the daily communication is necessary for managing the enterprise successfully.

Evaluative feedback puts the receiver into the spotlight; it is his or her qualities that are brought to light. With personal feedback, however, the sender is exposed just as much as the receiver, sometimes even more. For example, if you get irritated about a colleague being slipshod, that might also be seen as a manifestation of your own excessive meticulousness. By giving him feedback, you show your own need for orderliness and control, and you can expect to get feedback on that, yourself. Both perspectives are equally valid. Neither you nor your colleague is the source of the conflict caused by differences in attitude toward orderliness; rather, it emerges from the encounter of your personal preferences. Thus, by giving him personal feedback, you are inviting him to participate in a process of mutual exploration of how each of you impacts the other.

The quality of personal feedback depends on whether it is given with the best possible intentions, *i.e.,* with the purpose of contributing to the receiver's learning and growth. A good rule of thumb is: *What is said should be something the receiver needs to hear, not something that the sender wants to eliminate by projecting it onto the receiver.* Feedback built on projecting one's own undesired traits onto someone else, and then criticizing these traits as if they belong to that person, has no value whatsoever for the receiver. On the contrary, the receiver will have every reason to feel he has been used. (You can read more about the psychological defense mechanism of *projection* in Appendix, page 292).

Feedback with elements of deliberate manipulation or unconscious projection has a tendency to shift from being personal to becoming evaluative. The sender has no intention to have his own motives examined, so he holds the receiver fully responsible for what he has to say. When co-workers or managers on the same level give each other evaluative feedback, they run the risk of getting caught in an accusatory debate about whose perspective is "right," instead of involving themselves in a mutual process of exploring and learning. Objections against the content of the feedback is mixed with opposition against the other, who is seen as sitting in judgment of oneself. That is viewed as changing the symmetrical and equal relationship into one that is asymmetrical;[13] the deliverer of feedback will be suspected of trying to gain power by assuming a superior position. Among employees, such behavior is often met with: "Do you think you're the boss?" In many companies and organizations evaluative feedback is the only feedback given, since there is no knowledge and experience of any alternative. In such cases, no feedback at all is given among

---

[13] A paradoxical, but very powerful way to "psych out" an opponent when playing table tennis is to praise his or her playing. On the face of it, it's a positive reinforcement that stimulates him or her to perform better. On a more profound level, it is a way to redefine the symmetrical relationship between the players, by assuming the role of a "teacher" who is evaluating a less experienced "pupil." If the latter does not see through the trick, it will probably impair his playing.

peers. Instead, the boss or someone higher in the organization is supposed to take responsibility for correcting misbehavior and mistakes.

Furthermore, if feedback is used exclusively in its evaluative form, it will be seen as unnatural for any employee to express any feedback whatsoever to his boss. The superior, by right of his or her formal position, is expected to evaluate the subordinate, not the other way around. The drawback in this is that it increases the risk of managers being "isolated on the top," since they are deprived of the input they need to make good decisions and grow as leaders.

Unlike evaluative feedback, personal feedback is not necessarily restricted by the formal hierarchy of the organization. It is possible, and also desirable, to give feedback to your boss, sometimes even to other superiors with whom you have personal contact. Of course, the distribution of formal power cannot be disregarded, although it is not the most decisive factor. Of greater importance are the levels of openness and trust characterizing your relationship, and the corporate culture you share. It is a commonly held belief that managers have to keep a personal distance from their subordinates if they are not to lose their respect. I do not subscribe to this belief. In my opinion, if it is necessary for the boss to keep distance to maintain his or her integrity, that is a symptom of deficiencies in the corporate culture.

In the example above, from the management team of Company X, we can see how CEO Richard reacts with annoyance to feedback given to him. By testily defending himself using counterarguments, he responds to the personal feedback as if it were evaluative. His doing so can be regarded as a defensive maneuver, moving the issue to a realm where he, by virtue of his formal position, can expect to have some control over what is to be considered "right" or "wrong." As seen earlier, it is characteristic of him to use his power to protect himself from what he does not want to hear. As with most people who get defensive, he does this routinely and unconsciously. Since his behavior hampers his ability to cooperate with his subordinates, it is important to raise his awareness of it, enabling him to assume responsibility for the consequences of his behavior. That, however, implies him getting the very feedback he is so vigorously fighting against, and, therefore, this is the reason the consultants insisted he listen to the others without answering back. Their intention is to bring the feedback back into the personal realm.

That Richard was the first person to get into a tight spot can also be regarded as a healthy sign. Obviously, people around him are dissatisfied with his style of leadership. In a more dysfunctional team, the irritation over his behavior would probably be channeled through attacking the member with the lowest standing in the team. This defense mechanism is known as *displacement*, which means that hostility toward a specific person is redirected toward a less risky target. Displacement of aggression is a primary cause behind victimization and scapegoating as a means to dissolve inner tensions within teams. That this was not happening in Company X's management team, despite the obvious frustration among its members, is a mark of the well-developed personal maturity among the individual members. This leads to the conclusion that their difficulties to act efficiently as a team are probably a consequence of how they interact, not of some dysfunctional aspects of their personalities.

Moreover, the team members' reactions to Richard's leadership style are not merely caused by his touchiness; there is also a prevalent uncertainty about what role the management team is supposed to have in the decision-making process. The exchange of opinions between John and Richard, about whether leading through a team is a good idea (see above, p. 101) did not help much to clarify this issue. Instead of an earnest attempt to scrutinize pros and cons, it became a showdown in which John was challenging the authority of his boss. However, it demonstrated that not all team members subscribed to Richard's idea of how to work as a team. That was partly caused by Richard's own ambiguity when explaining how he wants to manage the company.

One of the reasons for recruiting Richard to Company X was to import a more modern leadership style. He regards himself a team-oriented leader, holding the management team up as a well-functioning decision-making machine with the participation of all its members. However, some of the team members seem to participate more than others. When it comes to important decisions, Richard usually uses John, the marketing manager, or Jane, the administrative manager, as a sounding board. He also has regular appointments with Robert, the production manager, mainly to discuss issues related to production, but also to ventilate general company matters. Nevertheless, he claims that the important decisions are made when the entire management team is gathered.

When the others were interviewed at the outset of the team development process, they initially confirmed Richard as being team-oriented. However, that picture was modified when the questions became more detailed. The general opinion then appeared to be that he likes making the decisions himself, then, afterward, trying to beguile the others into believing that they had really been part of the decision-making process. Mary expressed it this way:

"When Richard presents a matter to the team, he tries to make it sound as if it's open for decision, but soon you notice that he's already made up his mind about how to solve it. He's very clever at supporting ideas that support his own, and ignoring or rejecting those that don't. I think all of us have realized that we'd better agree with him, or perhaps suggest minor modifications. He'll get it his own way, anyhow."

John is often engaged as a sounding board for Richard but, nevertheless, he can also feel excluded from the real decision-making process:

"When discussing the reorganization of the company, we were all supposed to have impact on the final solution. I differed from the others about the interface between marketing and customer support, but I got the feeling that the issue was already settled." [Interviewer: "Settled in what way?"] "Well, Richard had spoken to Mary and talked her into supporting his view, and neither of them was interested in listening to any objections."

Susan, the personnel manager, said:

"I've noticed that every time I try to pursue a different point of view, it ends up with me getting more work to do….something to analyze or investigate and report back to the team. It makes me cautious to reveal a divergent opinion." [Interviewer: "Do they all respond that way?"] "Well, I guess it's mostly Richard."

When asked what Richard does to make them a real team, they answer that he has initiated several team-building activities, like white water rafting and paint-balling. He is also concerned about keeping a good atmosphere in the team, *i.e.*, by taking an after-work beer at least once a month. He always talks of the management in terms of "we." He's even been nicknamed, "Mr. Team" by people in the production department, after he enthusiastically endorsed teamwork at a department gathering.

His behavior is not unusual for managers who have participated in leadership training. He has understood the advantages of team-based leadership, and he knows that it calls for maintaining and advancing the team. However, he is unaware of how his espoused approach is undermined by his way of acting. In addition to that, his talking team and acting as a single-leader reinforces one of the main problems of Company X: *the "Talking-Doing" gap.* The fact that neither he nor the other team members is aware of this gap shows that it is an intrinsic element of the corporate culture. They are so habituated to these inconsistencies that they have ceased to reflect upon them. When asked during the interviews, they had no difficulties in seeing the contradiction, but no one seemed to take it seriously.

Another manifestation of the corporate culture in Company X is the cheerful tone in which the statements quoted above were spoken. Here, too, it took just a simple question from the consultants to make the interviewees realize that their criticism was, in fact, seriously meant. When they realized that, all three of them became eager to take the sting out of their statements by explaining it was no real problem, and that they had all the impact on the decisions that they wished.

The reactions described above illustrate another defensive pattern that is typical among the employees of Company X, managers as well as subordinates. At first you do not notice (that is, defensive unawareness); when what's unnoticed is brought to your attention, you do not take it seriously (isolation of affect); and when you realize that it is serious after all, you do what you can to play it down (undoing, rationalization).[14] It's quite understandable that many suggestions and solutions are choked by a defensive strategy like these.

Furthermore, the examples above point to an aspect that must be considered when making organizational reviews. The answer to a simple question can be misleading if one disregards how it is said, i.e., the affective expression, body language, and context in which it is delivered. Much information is embedded in dissonances and incongruities expressed during an interview. Information of that kind will inevitably get lost when standardized surveys are used.

Single-leader management or real management team? [15]

Of course, as we have seen, the idea of leading through a team raises several questions. Are there any benefits from doing so? Many successful management teams meet to share and discuss information, not to come to decisions through teamwork. Is it possible for a team to assume responsibility for important decisions? The top manager

---

[14] For further explanation of these defense mechanisms, see Appendix.

[15] These are terms used by Jon R. Katzenbach in his book, *Teams at the Top: Unleashing the Potential of Both Teams and Individual Leaders* (Cambridge, MA.: Harvard Business School Press, 1998).

of the team will be accountable, anyhow; why make it more complicated?

In single-leader management, the CEO (or, at lower levels, the top manager) sets goals and targets, and defines what measures to take. When needing support, advice, or just someone who will act as a sounding board, he turns to his boss, or, if he is the CEO, then to his Board of Directors. Occasionally, he uses smaller groups of subordinates to work through to his decisions, and the subordinate members of the management team will be held accountable for the execution of decisions made by the single leader. At best, the management team itself will serve as the sounding board, where the CEO and his direct reports can get input from the others before making their own decisions.

In a real management team, on the other hand, team members hold each other accountable for the performance of the whole team, as well as for how each member contributes to the success of their joint enterprise. The overall management issues are a concern for all team members. Consensus is worth aiming at, but not always attainable. The leader of the team still has the overall responsibility for decisions that are made, but he or she takes that on by securing the quality of the team's decision-making process.

Of course, this does not reduce the responsibilities of the heads of the departments for achieving results within their own realms. Responsibility is not a zero-sum game. In a real management team, responsibility for the totality is added to, and prioritized over, the existing responsibility for the team's part, but not replacing it.

The decision triangle

When a team must make a decision, there are three overall aspects that must be considered: *hastiness*, *quality*, and *commitment*. (See diagram 1, below.)

Hastiness is the time it takes to raise an issue and decide on a plan of action to carry it out. Note that this does not necessarily mean the action will be carried out in the shortest possible time. Rather, a hasty decision has a tendency to generate protracted implementation processes.

The *quality* of the decision depends on how much of the relevant information has been used in the decision-making process, and the acumen of team members who are using that information to form the best decision possible.

Commitment refers to team members buying into the decision, feeling fully responsible for launching it, and carrying it through. When referring to the decision, they use words like "we've agreed to" instead of "the management team has decided"; the latter is a subtle way of disowning responsibility by dissociating oneself from what has been decided.

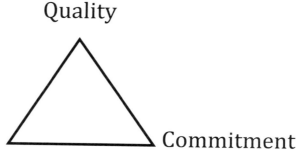

Diagram 1. The decision triangle

If a decision has to be made *hastily*, single-leadership is by far the most advantageous way to proceed. At any time, the single-leader can determine that he has enough information and take action directly. The process in a real management team is lengthier; everyone has to be informed of all aspects of the issue, and attaining a joint understanding of what to do is a time-consuming activity. In addition, it can be complicated by power struggles and personal conflicts.

Generally, the closer to the daily hands-on operations, the more need there is for hasty decisions. Machinists and sales people make hundreds of decisions every day without reflecting. At the management level, fast decisions are mostly called for when a crisis occurs. This creates a dilemma for the leader, since urgent situations make quality and commitment more necessary. For this reason, balancing the three aspects—hastiness, quality, and commitment—is a crucial leadership skill.

If *commitment* is the most important aspect for realizing a decision, a true leadership team is preferable. Involving the whole team in making the decision will increase the likelihood that all the members will back it up, verbally, as well as in action. Furthermore, the probability is increased that their subordinates will feel committed and obliged to carry out the decided actions as well, compared to how they will feel when their boss is just conveying a message from his, or her, superiors. Thus, commitment has a strong effect on the extent to which a decision is implemented in the organization, particularly when it comes to abstract issues like enforcing visions, values, and strategies. It is equally so for insuring that operational hands-on activities are performed with a minimum of delay.

When quality is the top priority, the choice between the two management types is less obvious. A real management team has a great potential for making high-quality decisions, especially when it comes to complex management issues with a high degree of uncertainty. However, the decision-making quality of the team is also dependent on the quality of their cooperation. An immature team cannot be expected to make better decisions than an experienced single-leader. Most people who have been part of a group that has struggled to decide something have experienced being prepared to accept any decision whatsoever just to put an end to an unavailing discussion. The wish for a strong single-leader is quite understandable in situations like that. Nevertheless, for securing high quality decisions in the long run, the quality brought into the process by a mature team of dedicated members is unbeatable.

Prerequisites for building a real management team

Katzenbach suggests four criteria that must be met in a real management team.[16] Together they form the *discipline of teams* that he considers essential for the team's ability to exceed the capability of one led by a single-leader. These criteria are:

A small number of members. The optimal team should not have more than 10 members. Larger groups can occasionally work as real teams, but they will generally perform better if they can break out into subgroups.

Complementary knowledge and skills. This means that team members jointly possess the knowledge and skills needed for accomplishing the team task. Three kinds of capabilities related to the purpose and goals of the team must be balanced: *technical and functional expertise, problem-solving and decision-making skills,* and *interpersonal (i.e., communication and cooperation) skills.*

Common purpose and common goals. A shared commitment to an urgent and worthwhile purpose, expressed in inciting goals, is necessary for a team to unleash its potential.

---

[16] See Katzenbach, J. , *ante.*

Commitment to a common approach. The team has to come to an agreement about how they will work together; who will be doing what; what individual skills are needed, and how they will be integrated together; how continuing membership in the team is to be earned; and how decisions will be made and modified.

Real management teams are quite rare, probably because very few managers know what it truly takes to make a team perform with excellence. There is a widespread belief that wise people coming together to achieve something will spontaneously form a wise group—this assumption is contradicted by experience, as well as by research, for example, Bion (1991)[17] and Belbin (2010). [18]

In fact, the ability to cooperate as a team is a competence in and of itself, distinct from the knowledge and skills needed to deal with "matter-of-fact" issues. This competence has been labeled *social competence* or *emotional intelligence*. However, combining emotionally intelligent people in a group is seldom enough to form an excellent team, especially in the long run. It also takes an assiduous effort to clear the communication channels from disturbances like hidden agendas, unresolved conflicts, and interpersonal tensions. Even if this can be done, it will not be sufficient; making it possible to give feedback and call for accountability will not guarantee this

---

[17] Bion, W. R., *Experiences in Groups* (London: Tavistock, 1961).

[18] Belbin, M., *Management Teams: Why They Succeed or Fail* (Oxford, UK: Routledge– Taylor & Francis, 2010).

possibility will be carried through in action. Consequently, Katzenbach's five criteria must be considered necessary but not adequate. In the following chapters, we shall consider the dynamics that are required for realizing a well-functioning management team.

As suggested above, the usefulness of a real management team, as defined by Katzenbach, depends on the purpose and aims of the team. The choice between single-leader management and a real team is also relevant to the corporate culture that top management wants to transmit to the rest of the organization. A top management team can be regarded as a generator of values, attitudes, and approaches. Their behavior will form a model for the entire organization, far more impactful than trumpeted verbal messages. This aspect must not be disregarded when forming a strategy for increasing profit and cutting costs.

Considering the situation of Company X and its shortcomings as described in chapter 2, there are good reasons to favor a real management team. The necessity for top management to strengthen its impact on the culture and way of doing things in the organization is reason enough, but, in order to put that into effect, they will first have to grow a competence for dealing with complex and emotionally challenging issues. It would be a good thing, then, if Richard can become more consequent in his ambition to lead through a real team. However, that by itself will not be enough without the other team members

also shouldering their responsibility for the decision process, as well.

> When the team members come together again
> after the break, there is an uneasy silence. Richard
> breaks it, saying: "I don't think we'll get any fur-
> ther tonight." Jane says she's having a headache
> and would prefer going to bed soon. John suggests
> they should make a move for the bar. "I'm sure
> we'll talk better after a couple of beers." Robert
> endorses John's proposal, saying, "We can't just
> sit like this, staring at each other." The others
> keep quiet.
>
> One of the consultants suggests that they should
> reflect, one at a time, over what has occurred over
> the course of the day. John looks as if he's about to
> raise an objection, but Mary forestalls him: "I think
> it's been a good day. A lot of things we've dodged
> before have been brought to light. I've been rather
> inactive myself, but I'll be on the ball tomorrow,
> I promise." Asked why she's been inactive she
> replies, "I feel that it's always me questioning how
> we behave as a team. I've quite enjoyed leaning
> back, listening to what someone else has to say."
> The others choose to accept Mary's making excuses,
> and Susan continues: "I think, too, it's been useful
> talking like we did today. We haven't really solved
> anything, have we, but it feels as if we are more
> open to each other. I think it was plucky of you,

Richard, to ask for feedback on your leadership the way you did." The others nod in agreement. No one corrects Susan's embellishing characterization of Richard's behavior; at this moment, it's more important to make him happy again.

Robert says that a lot of thoughts have been roused during the day, but he's not ready to share them with the others. Jay agrees it's been an arduous day, and he wishes they had made more progress. Victor says he's gotten a good feeling about what they are doing but can't explain why. Jane expresses uneasiness about what will happen tomorrow; there is a tension between the members of the team that's scaring her. Mark says, "Well, I guess this will turn out well in the end." Asked to clarify, he says something nebulous about it always being useful for people to speak out. The others let his noncommittal statement pass, since no one has the energy to draw his real views out of him. Richard says that the discussions certainly have been fruitful, but, at the same time, he implies that there are issues not dissected yet that might be more important. For example, he continues, after a short pause, to say that there has been too much "walling-in" and too little cooperation between departments. He has not raised the issue earlier because he has hoped the department managers would bring it up themselves. No one picks up the gauntlet, so he relapses into unfolding his thoughts about teamwork.

Finally, all but John have shared their reflections. John now says that he is surprised that all the others have had so much positive to say about today's work. As for himself, he's rather frustrated and confused, but he doesn't reveal that to the others. Instead, he says, "I guess this is okay, but far too sluggish for my taste. I can't see that we've accomplished anything at all." Susan looks at him with an amused smile. Victor asks her why she's smiling and, at first, she is reluctant to answer; then she turns to John, with: "Sometimes you remind me of my 14-year-old son. It's as if he has to be opposing, even when I know that deep down he agrees." Everyone is laughing, eventually even John. Richard says, "Let's head for the bar," and the team calls it a day. Jane goes to her room, but the rest of them follow Richard's invitation. Soon, Susan and John are involved in an animated discussion. Jay and Mary take seats at a table, talking tentatively about the events of today. The rest let their attention be caught by the screen above the bar, which is telecasting the latest sport news.

CHAPTER 5.
DEFENSIVE ROUTINES IN ORGANIZATIONS

So far, we have used the word *defensive* in several combinations: defensive patterns, defensive reactions, defensive maneuvers, and defensive routines. Now, it's time to take a comprehensive look at the phenomenon itself.

Defensiveness means being on one's guard, preventing, avoiding, or averting dangers. If we are physically attacked, we have the choice of protecting ourselves by trying to overpower the attacker or by running away. This impulse of "fight or flight" is automatically activated prior to any deliberate choice of how to handle the situation. It's a reflex we have in common with most living organisms.

However, it's not just our physical survival we are inclined to defend: preserving our *self-esteem* by maintaining a coherent and positive self-image is just as crucial for human beings. The threat against our image of ourselves can come from outside, for example, by indignities, disparaging comments, or by being caught acting in a socially inappropriate way. It can also come from within: intense feelings of shame, guilt, rage, and powerlessness are also severe threats against our self-esteem. Similar to when we experience physical threats, we evolve ways to fight, or flee from, these internal threats. We use the term *psychological defense mechanisms* to describe our ways of protecting ourselves (literally, *our selves*) against these internal threats. For example, we can disown responsibility for a situation we're involved in by *projecting* guilt onto someone else, or shut out the emotional aspects of the situation by using *intellectualization* and *isolation of affect*.[19]

By using defense mechanisms, we can maintain our mental balance in situations which otherwise would endanger our self-esteem. However, this will always be at the cost of a more or less distorted perception of reality, which, in turn, will be to the detriment of our ability to gain self-awareness. Since both deal with reality—physical as well as interpersonal—and self-knowledge is the determining factor for the ability to exercise leadership, exposing and reducing the use of defense mechanisms will be an important aspect of efficient leadership training.

We'll use the term "psychological defense mechanisms" exclusively for cases in which they are used unconsciously, which, in this context, means instinctively and unpremeditatedly. Deliberate blaming, denial, or back-stabbing will be referred to as manipulations. Sometimes,

---

[19] See Appendix.

however, it's hard to decide if it's one or the other we're dealing with. For example, you can be vaguely aware of projecting an undesired aspect of yourself onto a colleague but make a deliberate choice to keep doing that, instead of reflecting on your own responsibility.

Defense mechanisms on an organizational level

In groups, and in organizations, the defense mechanisms are elevated to a higher level of complexity, since they are both influencing and being influenced by the existing patterns of interaction. The distortion of reality caused by psychological defenses is reinforced by the resonance caused by people sharing and confirming the same delusions. When all group members are projecting their failures on circumstantial factors, there is no one to raise an opposing perspective that might restore a sense of reality. Instead, the distorted view becomes a self-reinforcing "truth," and an intrinsic element of the group culture. At the same time, aspects of reality threatening to deflate the shared beliefs must be kept away; the defensive patterns of behavior used within a group or an organization serves that purpose.

The former Harvard Business School professor Chris Argyris has dedicated much of his scientific research to understanding defensive organizational patterns. In *Overcoming Organizational Defenses,* he describes how these patterns emerge from people's habitual dealing with situations that might cause them to experience embarrassment or threat. By using the apposite expression *skilled incompetence*, he suggests that we are trained to wink at aspects of social reality that might put others or ourselves in an embarrassing situation. Furthermore, we develop *organizational defensive routines*, which help us bypass potentially embarrassing situations, and which cover up our doing so.[20] This bypassing and covering up is carried through by the use of *fancy footwork*, *i.e.*, "as-if" actions diverting attention from the defensive character of our behavior and from the consequences of it. Since these "as-if" actions do not address and solve the real problems of the organization, they contribute to a feeling of uneasiness and a sense of inability to do anything to reduce that feeling. Argyris uses the term *malaise* for this state of mind.

The outcome of this sequence of skilled incompetence ➔ defensive routines ➔ fancy footwork ➔ malaise is a general acceptance of mediocrity. Let's take a closer look at its elements.

---

[20] "Organizational defense routines are actions or policies that prevent individuals or segments of the organization from experiencing embarrassment or threat. Simultaneously, they prevent people from identifying and getting rid of the causes of the potential embarrassment and threat. Organizational defense routines are antilearning, overprotective, and self-sealing." Argyris, C., *ante*, p. 25.

Skilled incompetence

By using the term *skilled incompetence*, Argyris points to one of many paradoxes in organizational life. The word *skilled* implies ability acquired through purposeful training; in this case the *incompetence* is a direct effect of this training, as well as our lack of freedom to break the internalized regulatory system caused by it. The paradox can be phrased this way: the more socially competent we get, the more incompetent we'll be dealing with some of the important aspects of social reality. Argyris explains this paradox:

> "We can think of human beings as having been taught, early in life, how to act in ways to be in control, especially when they are dealing with issues that can be embarrassing or threatening. People transform these lessons into theories of action. The theories of action, in turn, contain rules that are used to design and implement the actions in everyday life." [21]

As human beings we feel good when we're in control of our actions and their consequences. Correspondingly, we abhor being out of control. Since, in embarrassing or threatening situations, we risk losing control, we learn early in life how to avoid them. One way to do so is to seek unilateral control—*i.e.*, to win, or, at least, to avoid

---

[21] Argyris, C., *ante,* p. 12.

coming into a disadvantageous position—and not to upset people.

However, when working closely with other people, it's futile to try and exert control over them while, at the same time, avoiding everything that might annoy them. This calls for strategies of bypassing unpleasant situations and, if that's not completely successful, of saving face. In such situations, keeping up appearances and covering up for each other becomes more important than facing reality. This face-saving cannot be done explicitly; if you tell someone you're saving his face, you're rather doing the opposite.[22] We must conceal what we do by using white lies, and we must also conceal that we are concealing it.

In the course of time, this defensive strategy becomes an integrated part of what we think of as our "social competence." Instinctively, we perform our practiced maneuvers of saving someone else's or our own face, and of concealing doing so. Eventually, our acquired social adaptability causes us to lose the ability to raise issues that might be unpleasant. The culture of social intercourse we've been part of creating gives no room for genuine sincerity, since that could put others, or us, in embarrassing situations. This also holds for those situations

---

[22] This can be illustrated by the very old story about how the diplomatic corpse dealt with the British Queen Victoria's habit of farting during cabinet meetings. The first time, the French ambassador left the room after saying, "Excuse me, my stomach isn't quite well today." The second time, the Italian ambassador rose, saying, "Accept my excuses, I must have eaten something I shouldn't"; then he also left. The third time, the German ambassador started up, proclaiming: "Great Empire of Germany accepts responsibility for this one and the three to follow."

when common sense indicates that absence of sincerity will result in worse discomfort in the long run. This attitude can also end up in disaster, as will be discussed later in this chapter.

We would probably have big trouble putting up with our skilled incompetence unless we also developed a *skilled unawareness,* wherein we stop noticing behavior, other's as well as our own, that, if noticed, would put someone in an awkward position. The unawareness is about what we conceal, but also about the fact that we are concealing it. As in the case of skilled incompetence, this is a genuine inability, not a deliberate attempt to disregard what's going on. It's not that we look the other way; we develop an *inattentional blindness*[23] to potentially embarrassing aspects of what's happening. This explains why it's so hard to change dysfunctional behavior patterns in a group of which one is a member. We just do not see what we're actually doing.

Our striving for not avoiding a disadvantageous position vis-à-vis others has further consequences, in addition to face saving and bypassing unpleasantness. In hierarchical organizations with strong internal competition—which is true for almost all organizations—the safest way not to come into a disadvantageous position is to aim for the opposite: being the top dog. This means putting the other in an underdog position, thus creating a win-lose situation. Since the other has the same ambition, both will

---

[23] I have borrowed the term from Ig Nobel Prize winners Daniel Simons and Christopher Chabris. See Simons, D. and Chabris, Ch., *The Invisible Gorilla: How Our Intuitions Deceive Us* (New York: Crown Publishing Group, 2010).

try to increase their own effectiveness at the cost of the other. This paves the way for another paradox: the more effective they try to be individually, the less effective they are together.

This is a parallel to a famous paradox: *the prisoners' dilemma*. Two prisoners are separately given this offer: if you both confess, both of you will get a very mild punishment. If both of you deny, both of you will get a severe punishment. If one of you confesses and the other denies, the confessor will get a very severe punishment and the other will be released.

This dilemma emanates from the outcome of my choice being dependent on the plea of my fellow prisoner. If I confess for the sake of us both, how can I be sure that he doesn't take a chance on getting released, putting me in prison forever? If I deny, I might get released, but I also risk being severely punished if he denies, too. Thus, I'm dependent on his ability to reason in a similar way, and his having both our best interests in mind. If I am to choose what's best for us both, I have to trust him to make the same choice.

People fighting for power and influence in a management team face a situation very similar to the prisoners' dilemma. It takes a great deal of mutual trust to give up unilateral control and other manipulations intended to maximize one's own benefits, and, instead, to make oneself vulnerable by lowering her guard, and, thereby, make genuine cooperation possible.

The manipulative behavior sprung from skilled incompetence and skilled awareness is a poor basis for building mutual trust. Face saving doesn't help either; smoothing the other person's defeat is just a more subtle way of confirming one's own top-dog position and has nothing to do with genuine care for the other.

Management team members' attempts to gain unilateral control over each other contribute strongly to sub-optimizations referred to as "lack of overall responsibility" and "siloing." The power struggle makes it totally rational to protect one's own territory and to look at invitations to cooperation with suspicion, since manipulative maneuvers by others, as well as by oneself, have a good chance of being successful, due to a lack of attention to the interpersonal dynamics.

It's a well-known fact that power struggles like this are the source of inefficiency in many companies and organizations. The problem is, partly, an undesired side effect of promoting competitive people to leading roles. Making a career in a company means competing with colleagues in an apparent win-lose situation, where the win-win outcome of the prisoners' dilemma isn't an option. It's tempting to use dirty tricks, like backbiting, withholding information, or putting a wrench in the works for potential competitors for a desired promotion. This is easily done in low-trust and low-transparency organizations, since they tend to foster the "skilled unawareness" described above, making it possible to manipulate under the radar. Internal competition is no big problem if it is open and transparent, thus making it possible for everyone to see that the best man or woman was promoted, and not the one who is most skilled in foul play.

In addition to that, there is another reason for curbing the proclivity for internal competition among B and C level managers. The visionary and culture-building leadership at the top of the pyramid differs considerably from leading an operational part of its base. In the latter case, beating your colleagues can be inspirational; in the former it will be devastating for management's ability to implement its strategies. Mature leadership means being aware of when competition boosts efficiency and when it does the opposite.

Defensive routines

Our "skilled" inability to take the bull by the horns by raising controversial issues compels us to find ways to get around them. When this dodging turns into established organizational practice, we call it *defensive routines*. The word "routines" suggests that we are talking about ingrained habitual patterns that have become an everyday element of interpersonal behavior.

Defensive routines serve a bypass function, circumventing issues that are difficult to deal with, either because they are unpleasant and/or embarrassing, or so complicated that people cannot solve them without taking the risk of exposing their ignorance or insecurity. As suggested above, for a bypass operation of this kind to be successful, it has to be concealed, and the fact that it is concealed has to be concealed, too. Due to this three-step lock-up, addressing the real problems in an organization with well-developed defensive routines will be perceived as difficult, or even pointless. Consequently, urgent organizational change is not initiated, or, if it is anyway, it isn't carried through efficiently. Furthermore, a defensive top management team spreads a defensive culture throughout the organization, and since culture is usually taken for granted, as the water is for the fish, this contributes to making the defensive routines imperceptible.

For actions to be called defensive routines, they must turn into coherent patterns of behavior that are characteristic for the organization's way to handle reality. These manifest expressions of defensiveness show a vast variety within and between organizations, many of which can be classified into either of two main categories: structural solutions to dynamic problems; and contradictory messages that must not be questioned.

Structural solutions to dynamic problems

A common way of dealing with—i.e., bypassing—conflicts and other cooperation difficulties is reshaping the formal organizational structure. If two managers within a department do not get along well, you can split their unit into two, minimizing their encounter by letting their work be coordinated by their joint boss. Occasionally, even new departments are established to give a manager with difficulties in cooperating with others a turf of his own where he doesn't have to fray on colleagues.

The positive effects of defensive reorganizations, if any, are seldom lasting; the underlying conflicts usually find new arenas in which they can be enacted. This way of handling them will also give rise to new problems. Management's credibility will be undermined when its inability to solve their internal problems is exposed to the rest of the organization. It also reduces the legitimacy of necessary reorganizations due to changes in the market. In addition to that, the sub-optimization on the top level sanctions similar inefficient and conflict-avoiding actions throughout the organization.

In everyday organizational life, we can find more common and less dramatic examples of trying to solve interpersonal dynamics problems by the use of structural changes. This is one example:

A project team of a telecom company worked with a customer to create a technical solution. The team had several meetings with representatives of the client to specify what and when to deliver. Both parts found the meetings positive and forthright, and all were satisfied with the outcome. However, after those meetings, it became clear that the project team members had different images of what had been agreed upon and of what the client really wanted. Therefore, they were compelled to address the client for clarifications, which caused the client's representatives to report that they had a lurking feeling they had not really gotten through to the project team after all.

The project team's conclusion after this follow-up was that the project model they used was not fine-tuned enough to catch the subtleties of the customer's needs. Therefore, they spent time and money refining the project model before the next client meeting. However, the same thing happened the second time: everyone was satisfied at the end of the meeting, but obscurities were discovered afterward. The team's conclusion was also the same: we have to make the project model even more detailed.

It is quite obvious that the problem wasn't the project model; rather it was an insufficient connection between customer representatives and project team members. This course of events illustrates a typical feature of teams with too-shallow interpersonal relations. They had a feeling of being in agreement, when they were, in fact, uncertain of exactly what they were in agreement about. This discrepancy is caused by everyone filling in the blanks of information with assumptions of their own. These assumptions tend to get biased by wishful thinking and personal needs. The tech geek "hears" that the technique has to be refined; while the market guy "hears" that his realm should be given more priority, etc. The lack of an explorative group climate leads to these assumptions not being tested against reality.

Instead of looking for solutions in the structural framework, the team members could have asked themselves: What is it about our team that prevents us from exploring the customer's needs to the bottom? One possible answer to that question might be: To know, I'll have to raise questions, thus showing my ignorance. In this team, no one wants to show weakness by being ignorant, so we don't ask questions if that can make us look stupid; and since we don't know beforehand what might be seen as stupidity by the others, we are generally cautious about raising questions. Our general cautiousness prevents us from both getting full information and from attaining the personal contact with the client representatives that is necessary for us to understand each other.

The latter problem description highlights qualities like openness, trust, closeness, and emotional contact, having in common that a project model, no matter how circumstantial, cannot guarantee them. Rather, to deal with them, one has to treat the team as a self-regulating social system, whose team members are able to influence the unspoken regulatory system defining what is acceptable to say and do. To do this, they have to achieve competence to create and maintain sufficient quality of the working process, *i.e.,* the same competence that the management team of Company X is now about to acquire.

There are many similar examples from companies, as well as from public organizations. Here is another:

The top management team of a public organization had severe difficulties making decisions and implementing decided measures. After the management team meetings, many of the members had a feeling of not having been given an opportunity to express their opinion. Most of the management issues were dealt with in informal meetings at which two or three team members were present, which solved the cooperation problem momentarily; in the long run, however, the lack of efficiency was aggravated, since few of the team members were committed to following the resolutions decided in these meetings. The rest of the organization reacted to the conflicting messages from top management with a general feeling of dejection, resulting in declining performance.

In an attempt to cope with these problems, the team spent two days off-site, aiming to agree on a "code of conduct" for team meetings. The members took on the task enthusiastically, and after two days of animated discussions, committed themselves to a list of six rules: state your opinion; ask if you don't understand; give feedback to other team members; acknowledge different opinions, but be loyal to joint decisions; and two more. In order to enforce the rules, these were printed on the agenda, insuring that all team members had them right under their noses.

The first team meeting after the offsite was carried out in good spirit. Everyone was convinced they could speak freely, even if no one dared to challenge the situation by fully using the rules of the code. At the second meeting, a slight feeling of discouragement had crept into the team; at the third meeting, it became obvious that they had reverted to the dysfunctional behavior before the offsite. They kept the six rules of conduct on their printed meeting agendas, but no one pointed to the apparent contrast between what was written and their manifest behavior.

The measure that the management team was taking—committing themselves to a code of conduct—seems quite reasonable. I have asked many colleagues and most of them say that a two-day workshop on rules of conduct is exactly what they would prescribe for a team like this. Yet, the treatment was totally ineffective. How can that be explained?

Some simple checkout questions might have been enough to reveal the futility of the measure taken. "Which of the rules agreed on are new to you? Didn't you already know that they should be followed before coming to this workshop?" After answering the second question in the affirmative, which they likely would, they might redirect their attention to *why* they act as they do. This implies leaving the rather pleasant task of listing wished-for behavior for something much more challenging: to evaluate what they actually were doing and how they felt doing it. This means addressing and dealing with feelings of fear, anger, disappointment, and dejection, *i.e.,* the emotional dynamics propelling the interaction of the team. It was the projected unpleasantness of such an approach that made the management team grasp an easier way out.

The case above illustrates why leadership training so often fails to deliver intended effects on leadership behavior. The wish to avoid anything that might be uncomfortable—feelings, for example—paves the way for rationalistic, simplistic, and "positive" approaches. It's like papering a rotten wall, hoping that the putrefaction will disappear if ignored, or like filling a tooth cavity without drilling to remove the decay area in a misdirected wish to spare the patient pain. Since structural aspects serve this purpose better than the unruly dynamic ones, they probably will continue to be preferred by leadership training purchasers, despite their inability to address the real problems.

Contradictory messages that must not be questioned

Another main category of defensive routines is based on using contradictory messages. The logic behind the routine can be described as follows:

1. Craft messages that contain inconsistencies.
2. Act as if the messages are not inconsistent.

3. Make the ambiguity and inconsistency in the message undiscussable.
4. Make the undiscussabilty of the undiscussable also undiscussable.[24]

The sequence above is known as *double bind*.[25] The term has its origin in family psychology, where it is used for a mentally disturbed parent inhibiting his or her child's development toward independence by giving contradictory messages. For example, the parent can say, "Give mummy a hug," and, at the same time, display a rejecting body language. The child's response is "wrong," no matter what it is. The double bind is effective because the child, due to the strong ties to the parent, is trapped in the situation and has no way to escape it.

Elements of the double bind can also be found in normal families, although in a less extreme form. Most children learn not to challenge mixed messages coming from adults, since doing so will generally evoke strong reactions. This lesson is a cornerstone in the pattern of social virtues mentioned earlier as *skilled incompetence*. The effectiveness of the double bind maneuvers in organizations is due to this skilled incompetence, and the fundamental emotional conditions are present: power, dependence, and need to be recognized and acknowledged.

---

[24] Argyris, C., *ante,* p. 27.

[25] Bateson, G., *Steps to an Ecology of Mind: Collected essays in Anthropology, Psychiatry, Evolution, and Epistemology* (Chicago: University of Chicago Press, 1972).

In chapter 4, we could see how the management team members of Company X sent contradictory signals when communicating with each other. Incongruences like that can have two, seemingly contradictory, consequences. If leadership is weak, as it will be with a leader exerting laissez-faire leadership style, subordinates are given the opportunity to choose which of the inconsistent signals to comply with. As a consequence, everyone prioritizes personal preferences, doing what's interesting or comfortable and neglecting tasks of more importance for company success. However, in an authoritarian climate, the effect seems to be the opposite: subordinates have to find out what management really wants, or, rather, what actions might get punished. The room for action gets limited to doing what surely will not get one in trouble. No initiatives will be taken, and the motivation for good performance will cease.

The most common form of contradictory messages is when what is said is inconsistent with what is expressed in action. Countless visions, policies, and good intentions have been thwarted by not being consistently backed-up in action. It is not unusual, therefore, that actions obviously countering espoused policies will be overlooked, with no one raising a finger to question them.

The destructivity of these discrepancies is due to organization cultures—norms of desirable, acceptable, or undesired behavior—being upheld far more by actions than by words. That's especially true for actions performed by top managers. The slightest disparity between their words and their actions can be used by anyone in the organization as a justification for being defensive, inefficient, and driven by self-interest rather than for attention to company success. Thus, a top management team lacking attention to how well their actions are in accordance with their words will be unable to fulfill one of their most important responsibilities, to create and maintain a corporate culture that is favorable for attaining core company goals.

Examples of words and actions pointing in different directions are ubiquitous in the organizational world. The management team committing themselves to a code of conduct was used above as an example of a structural solution to a dynamic problem, but it also exemplifies how agreements can be suspended when no one puts them into action. Here is another example:

A service company spent a great deal of time and money improving their brand. It was perceived by its customers as a bunch of competent but sluggish and boring nitpickers, an image with which they were, not surprisingly, reluctant to be associated. To alter that image, they choose a branding strategy, depicting the company as "your partner in an exciting world." This slogan spread fast in the company, mainly because all managers were charged with explaining and gaining support for the new strategy to their direct reports. Most of them liked the idea of becoming more exciting and dynamic, to fit the new company image. Yet, someone suggested that all employees should be offered a personal growth program, and that idea was turned down as too expensive. The same thing happened with a suggestion to brush up the dreary office furnishing. However, it was decided that all staff having direct contact with customers should attend a two-day course on "service management."

Six months later, the outcome of the new strategy was evaluated. The result was discouraging. A few customers had a slightly more positive impression of the company, but most of them did not. This called for a deeper analysis, and a consultant was brought in to interview the employees about what had gone wrong. The interviews revealed that management's presentation of the exciting future was so dull that the project had been doubted from the start. No change of behavior from the part of top management could be seen on other occasions either, which made the new slogan ring empty. On top of that, innovative initiatives taken by those having direct customer relations were choked, since their bosses felt uncomfortable approving untested approaches without asking their superiors. The formalistic structure and climate, together with a spirit of accuracy and cautiousness, made all such issues a concern for the top management team. And since the top management team meetings were held infrequently, the innovative ideas languished before they had a chance to get properly evaluated.

The lesson from this example is quite simple: a management team will not be able to implement a radical change of corporate culture unless they take it on themselves, shown by their decisions, actions, and interactions being consistently aligned with the new culture. This is why a successful change process has to start with a thorough processing of attitudes and defensive routines in the top management team.

A third category of contradictory messages consists of *verbal messages contradicting each other*. These are less usual than the other two types described above, probably because we are more attentive to what people say than to what they do, making it harder to get away with using verbal contradictions for the purpose of manipulation. However, a person trapped in the emotional straightjacket of the double bind (see above, p. 146) will be compelled to treat obviously contradicting messages as if they were not so. A crafty way to exercise power is to give contradictory orders; by putting the other in a situation where he will fail no matter what he does, the more powerful part is getting a hold over the other.

The mixed messages in an organizational context are usually less dramatic, but, even so, they can be devastating for motivation and performance. A boss can give ambiguous instructions deliberately or unconsciously, giving himself the freedom to act one way or another, or not at all. Possessing the interpretative prerogative due to his superior position, he can always save his own neck by blaming poor results on his subordinates.

Some contradictory messages are logical paradoxes, commonly known as "Catch 22's." Consider this example:

The following sentence is false. The previous sentence is true.

If the second sentence is false, the first has to be false, too, but that means that the second must be true, which means that the first sentence has to be true, etc. The novel and movie, "Catch 22," by Joseph Heller, gives many examples of how paradoxes of this kind cause deadlocks, making any change impossible.

The non-linear systemic quality of organizations and other systems of human interaction makes such paradoxes ubiquitous. *The openness-trust paradox*, basically a version of The Prisoners' Dilemma (see p. 136), is one example: I want to be open to you, but since openness is risky without mutual trust, I get cautious. I want you to open up first, so I'll be spared taking that risk by taking the first step. But since you think the same way, we are both cautious and, involuntarily, we're nurturing the mistrust that both of us want to get rid of.

The level of openness and trust is a very strong determinant of team and organizational functioning; it will be discussed in detail in chapter 6.

Other paradoxes arise when a manager is trying to adopt a non-authoritarian and empowering leadership style without really believing that his or her subordinates will shoulder the responsibility. It often ends up with a leadership style characterized by vaguely expressing disapproval afterward rather than giving distinct directions beforehand. The direct reports to such a boss will soon learn to avoid taking initiatives, because they will never know how their boss might react to them. The intention of the boss is to empower her subordinates, but the effect turns out to be the opposite. The less authoritarian the boss tries to be, the more dependent of her authority her direct reports become.

Vague and contradictory messages are quite suitable for building and maintaining defensive routines, mainly because they loosen up the distinct meaning of words, which blurs the conception of the reality they are supposed to describe. They create impenetrable smoke screens and twilight zones, which hide all sorts of inefficient or even destructive behavior. At the same time, they run counter to another human need: avoiding uncertainty. Accordingly, maintaining the defensive routines demands diverting attention from the blurred messages and directing it to another focus. That is the topic of the following section.

Fancy footwork

The previous section described how defensive routines are used to bypass what might lead to losing face or control. *Fancy footwork* takes the defensive routines one notch further, protecting them from being exposed by diverting attention to somewhere else. In this way, people involved escape getting their actions scrutinized by others, as well as by themselves, making it possible to disregard inconsistent actions and to deny the existence of these inconsistencies. If reality catches up after all, the possibility still remains of blaming both the inconsistencies and the covering them up on someone else.

A common way of keeping up appearances and covering up the lack of real progress is using grandiose language and window dressing. The pompous words and impressive images catch the attention of people and takes their focus from the fact that crucial issues are being bypassed and overlooked instead of dealt with. In some cases, a defensive maneuver is redefined into a wise or audacious venture by the use of bombastic rhetoric.

Other manifestations of fancy footwork are less obvious, making them even more effective as means to conceal indolence and defensiveness. Let's look at two types, both of frequent occurrences in organizations: positive jargon and slogans devoid of obligation; and describing shortcomings and incapacities as if they were virtues.

Positive jargon and slogans devoid of obligation

This category includes much of what has been called "corporate bullshit," i.e., embellishing trivial matters by the use of high-flown or sophisticated lingo. I will not go deeper into that, since it has been thoroughly described elsewhere.[26] Moreover, a list of these faddish expressions will probably get obsolete faster than it took this book to hit the market. For example, consider the slogan: Our people are our most important asset. When fresh, it infuses pride and hope into employees; today it might give rise to mockery, especially from the countless employees still waiting for their management to give substance to the fine words.

Other expressions of defensiveness are more mundane, which, in fact, makes them more insidious. As in the slogans above, the words are intended to point to one aspect of a phenomenon in order to conceal another. They often take the form of a description used as an incantation, routinely repeated without consideration. These descriptions become part of the self-image of the team or the organization. Let's look at two of the phrases I have picked up from organizations with which I have been working:

Everyone is free to speak his mind here. This is frequently said in organizations wanting to be looked upon as having an open and outspoken culture. However, that

---

[26] See, for example, Irwin, M., *The Ridiculous Business Jargon Dictionary: The world's most cringe-worthy business jargon, disambiguated.* © 2014 Matthew R. Irwin.

statement is very rare if it is actually true, *i.e.,* for organizations or teams where questioning, exploring, and spontaneity is, in fact, an everyday way of life. The need for pointing out that freedom to speak is unrestricted seems to decrease when it becomes a reality, making it more of an incantation than a reality statement, especially as it is not subject to any examination. On the contrary, there usually is an unspoken demand not to risk the good atmosphere by taking the statement literally.

The defensive quality will be confirmed if the statement is specified. "I can talk with my boss about everything"—but I withhold criticism, and I don't tell him what might backfire at the next wage review. "We don't mince words in the management team"—but we bypass issues that might cause irritation and avoid showing weaknesses that might be used for someone to increase his or her power. "We're good at giving each other positive feedback"—but we never actually do it. "I'm open for criticism," when everybody knows that the person saying so will use all his power to punish anyone who touches on his sore points.

There's a lot of ribbing here, but no harm is meant. This and similar phrases are commonly used by people describing and justifying the harsh jargon they use at work. To an outsider, such a jargon will sound like plain nastiness; among workmates, though, there is an unspoken agreement that the gibing is not to be taken as such, but rather as a token of them liking each other.

Superficially, some benefits come from using this kind of rough frankness. This harsh-sounding ribbing diverts and/or channels tensions that, otherwise, might cause conflicts. This deflection, known as *catharsis*, is similar to the psychological defense mechanism *displacement*.[27] If you are frustrated by your boss's behavior, you might find it too risky to address your anger toward him or her; instead, you pick a less challenging target to take it out on. Protected by the jargon, you can snap at a workmate who, in accordance with the unwritten rule, is not to take it personally. This safety valve helps prevent your not getting caught in personal disagreements, which makes it possible to concentrate on the task instead.

However, at a closer scrutiny, some of the disadvantages of jargon like this become clear. The possibility of stress relief by letting the frustration out in small doses might be seen as a blessing, but, at the same time, it deflates the motivation to address the cause of the frustration. If it is a symptom of inefficiency or lack of commitment, little is gained in the long run by keeping it on a bearable level. The underlying problems do not disappear by alleviating the symptoms, no matter how efficiently it's done. It is, metaphorically, as if scratching a tumor under the skin instead of having it removed.

Another drawback with using jargon is that no one has to take responsibility for what he or she says. When such an attitude is accepted regarding the ways people talk to

---

[27] From the Greek word *catharsis,* meaning purification of the soul. The defense mechanism displacement is also described in Appendix, p. 291.

each other, it will easily spread to other aspects of organizational life, making irresponsibility justifiable there, too. This adds to the invisible wall that anyone who wants to deal with the real issues has to break through, paving the way for more frustration, cynicism, and resignation.

In addition, jargon makes it easier to bully a workmate without having to stand up for doing so. The step from giving spiteful remarks for fun to being nasty for real becomes very small, making it possible to do the latter while claiming to do the former. He who takes offense is made responsible—"Can't you take a joke?"—not the offender. Thereby, the stronger and more ruthless person is given the interpretative prerogative over the one who is uncomfortable with the harsh language. When a team feels the need to have a scapegoat, there is a risk that the jargon will conceal the expulsion process until it cannot be reversed.

Jargon contributes to fancy footwork by sanctioning contradictory messages. An interaction culture, where "you f***ing idiot" can be translated into "I really like you," makes it easier to use words for manipulation than one where every syllable is taken seriously. Furthermore, the apparent outspokenness conceals that this "as-if" openness actually creates distance between people rather than closeness. Many have testified that the jargon they used to enjoy at work became a barrier to genuine contact with workmates when they were dealing with a crisis. Personal distance and lack of sincerity pave the way for defensiveness and fancy footwork. The temporary feeling of freedom coming from using a ruthless jargon is an illusion. In reality, everyone is trapped in a ritual, serving nothing but defensive purposes.

Describing shortcomings and incapacities as if they were virtues

In chapter 1, p. 6, we could see how John, the marketing manager of Company X, referred to himself as being *goal-oriented* when he was frustrated by the team groping its way to coping with the situation. Instead of talking about his inability to bear uncertainty and complexity, and about his fear of losing control, he hides his shortcomings by picturing himself as a person acting according to strong and positive virtues. We've also seen *matter-of-fact* orientation used in a similar way. Both ways are very efficient as means to make a team bypass unpleasant issues, especially ones involving emotions and doubt. By indirectly marking them insignificant, and dealing with them as signs of weakness, ignoring them becomes the appropriate thing to do.

Paradoxically, a defensive focusing on results can be an obstacle to attaining them. John's headstrong clinging to a role he is comfortable with is strongly contributing to the deadlock that immensely frustrates him. This is not the first time he blocks attempts from the other team members to dig deeper into a complicated problem. His insidious and moralizing way of trying to blame the others for the predicament contributes to the team being stuck. The implied accusation that the others do not have what it takes to achieve good results lures them into a defensive mode of action, either pretending not to catch the accusation or trying to refute it by promoting premature decisions. The alternative, *i.e.,* to search into the deeper meaning of John's statement, would take more openness and trust than the team has at this moment.

It would be unfair to accuse everyone who talks about him or herself as being goal-oriented, or matter-of-fact-oriented, of being defensive; of course, it can also be an accurate self-description. However, people highly focused on reality and really getting things done usually have little need for trumpeting that; they let their accomplishments speak for them. Rather, it's those who fail to attain excellent results who try to inflate their image by advertising themselves. An indirect and subtler way to do so is to take the role of the person pointing out and condemning the faults of others. If an employee is caught doing something unethical or illegal, you can often notice that some person distinguishes himself by getting far more upset and unforgiving than others. When asked, this person would refer to his most profound values of honesty having been offended by the outrageous behavior. However, if the basis of this moralistic attitude is scrutinized instead of taken at its face value, it quite often reveals that the moralizer has similar or worse deeds on his conscience.

The psychological dynamics behind such an attitude is well known. I disown aspects of my personality that

I cannot tolerate and *project*[28] them onto people around me. From that perspective, condemning those people is a way for me both to control my own impulses and to reinforce my denying having them. The more rabidly a person advocates honesty, morality, and ethics, the more the contrary will be found if someone takes the trouble to look behind the mask of self-righteousness.

As shown above, result-oriented and matter-of-fact-oriented are very usable expressions for describing short-comings as if they were virtues, but they are not the only ones. Energetic might mean that I get lost in complicated discussions, or that I am incapable of thinking strategically. People-oriented might be used to cover up a lack of determination or inability to push toward company goals. Faithful to company core values can sometimes be read as reluctance of adapting to change. The list of examples is much longer.

"Ruthless consideration"

Finally, let's look at a way of reasoning that is very common in teams having adopted personal feedback as a development tool. If explicitly put into words, it might be expressed: *Because of respect and consideration for you, I don't tell you what I really think about your behavior.* This does not quite fit into the category of fancy footwork, but it has several features similar to those in the examples above: hiding a motive sprung from fear and uncertainty

---

[28] The psychological defense mechanism *Projection* is explained in Appendix, p. 292.

behind an espoused motive sprung from virtue; operating by shaming and imposing guilt; and prioritizing face-saving over attaining excellent performance.

Though this way of thinking is seldom verbalized in the situation when feedback actually is given, it usually transpires when the difficulties of giving personal feedback is put on the agenda. In a working climate of mistrust and defensiveness, it is felt as too risky to criticize someone, since no one can be sure that the receiver will not find a treacherous way to get back at the sender of the feedback.

Since no one can question the praiseworthiness of being respectful and considerate, it will be seen as tactlessness to probe the defensive quality of the statement. The person doing so will not be looked upon as weak, as is the case when a claim to be result-oriented is questioned, but as an insensitive brute causing bad mood and psychological suffering. Shame and guilt are strong regulators of social behavior, making the slightest suggestion that someone is to blame for something very useful for defensive purposes, especially when that someone can be accused of causing emotional pain.

A colleague of mine once coined an apt expression for this attitude: ruthless consideration. The consideration part is obvious: sparing someone what might be painful. The ruthlessness of it, on the other hand, is often overlooked. By exempting someone from the lesser evil of getting hurt, we expose him to a worse evil: risking screwing up or becoming a nuisance without being given

a fair chance to correct his behavior. We would never subject people we really care for—our children for example—
to such a peril.

Malaise

The temporary relief brought by the defensive routines and
the fancy footwork comes at a bitter price. Contradictions,
prevarications, and "as-if" actions—made by others as
well as oneself—form an impenetrable web, dimming the
ongoing reality. Anyone trying to shed light on what's
actually happening will face the forces maintaining the
defensiveness in the form of disapproval, blaming, or
unsympathetic eyes. Moreover, a moment later, the victim
of this discipline might be one of the perpetrators correcting another group member's violation of the defensive norm. A pattern is, thus, cemented where everyone
engages in killing the initiatives taken by another member
of the group, in spite of everyone wishing the opposite.

This pattern is typical for defensive corporate cultures
that maintain the status quo. It generates a general feeling
that any attempt to change the state of things is mean-
ingless, unless one has total control over all parameters
determining the outcome. This feeling is the breeding
ground of hopelessness, cynicism, dissociation, and lack
of self-esteem, also known as learned helplessness.[29] The

---

[29] Learned helplessness can be exemplified by an experiment from the early
1950s. A pike is kept in an aquarium for the purpose of eating small fish
that are dropped in. One day, the experimenter puts a glass partition in the

disbelief in the possibility of having an influence on the working climate is based on experience. New employees with fresh ideas who have repeatedly faced a wall of unsympathetic reactions, soon learn that challenging the existing culture is fruitless. Hence, they become part of that same wall of reactions that will discourage subsequent new employees from expressing innovative ideas.

The inclination to blame others for things that go wrong will also increase, because, in the long run, it will be too heavy a burden to shoulder the responsibility for being part of the problem. Instead, the organization, the company, or the management is blamed, without the one casting the blame feeling any responsibility for changing the situation. For example, he or she can assert that it is useless to give feedback to management without having made any attempts whatsoever to do so. Furthermore, exaggerating the negative aspects of the organization, or of superiors, will make it easier for the individual to blame his own shortcomings on circumstances beyond his control.

This spiral of downheartedness cements the dysfunctional dynamics, which is detrimental both to

---

aquarium, confining the pike to one half of it. The small fish are put in the other half. The pike, seeing his supposed dinner through the glass, tries to snap it, and bangs his head against the glass wall every time. Eventually, he gives up trying to catch the small fish. Then, the experimenter removes the glass partition, making the small fish reachable again, but the pike makes no attempt to eat them. The glass confinement has become internalized in his brain, forcing him to give up catching them before even trying.

This experiment can be seen at: https://www.youtube.com/watch?v=Q6pWdIjAdn8

organizational goal-fulfillment and to employee well-being. Mystifying expressions like "It's just in the atmosphere" or "It's as much a part of the company as the bricks and mortar" completes the deadlock by both expressing and justifying inability to do anything about it.

The first step toward a changed corporate culture is to acknowledge that it has nothing to do with atmosphere, bricks and mortar, or other factors exerting mystical influence. It is all about the people involved and the self-reinforcing interactive dynamics they keep up. Only when they have realized that their behavior is very much a part of the problem, and they have the courage to challenge the unspoken rules maintaining the defensiveness, will they be able to break the vicious circle.

Mediocre performance

The sequence *skilled incompetence* > *defensive routines* > *fancy footwork* > *malaise* causes the organization to be deprived of necessary instruments for spurring excellent performance. An employee in a big company expressed it as follows:

> "It's useless trying to do an excellent job here; no one gives you any credit. My boss thinks it's okay, but that doesn't show in the pay envelope. The other guys in my department come up with jokes about brown-nosing if I try to do my best, but I have a feeling that it's more than a joke. Besides,

if I'm to do a good job I'll need much more support from people in other departments, but I don't
know who to talk to for making that happen. I do
as most of us: mind my own business and look for
job adverts."

The mediocrity adds fuel to the defensive routines and to
the reluctance to deal with them, which is no problem for
those who lack ambition. They can keep up an easy life
within the organization, and also find the argument that
justifies their doing so. It's much worse for those who
have a genuine wish to perform well and grow personally. Being part of a situation that runs counter to deeply
held values causes inner conflicts that can be detrimental
to one's mental health. This is particularly true for those
who do not have getting another job as a realistic option.

Defensive routines as the cause of disaster: The Challenger and Columbia space shuttles

Defensive routines are ubiquitous in companies, as well
as in public organizations. Nevertheless, I have chosen
the space shuttle accidents in 1986 and 2003 to exemplify
how these routines can pave the way for a disastrous outcome. The reason for doing so is the brilliant and exhaustive accident reports that describe the course of events
leading to the accidents. Both reports, the Columbia
Accident Investigation Board *Final report*, Chapters 7-8,

in particular, can be strongly recommended to anyone who wants to study organizational dynamics.

Challenger, 1986

The space shuttle Challenger disaster occurred on January 28, 1986, just after lift off from Kennedy Space Center in Florida, killing all seven members of the crew. The accident report[30] gives a detailed account of the technical flaws that caused the catastrophe: some rubber O-rings were not fit for the cold weather on the day of the launch.

The report also raises the question of why no one drew attention to the technical deficiencies so that the lift off could have been aborted. The answers they found can be summarized into four points:

- The problems with the O-rings were fully known by the engineers, but that knowledge stayed within the group and had no impact on the people in charge of the launch;
- Due to the strict hierarchical organization at NASA, it was not natural for a single engineer to comment on the project as a whole;
- A "can-do" attitude at all levels of the task at hand led everyone to focus on operational objectives; and
- The political pressure on the project management to launch without delay was strong.[31]

---

[30] Report of the Presidential Commission: *On the space shuttle Challenger accident.* (Washington, D.C.: Government Printing Office, June 5, 1986).

[31] *Ibid.,* chapter 5—my summary.

The Space Shuttle Project organization was based on a strict distribution of work tied together by an extensive report system. All disturbances threatening the time schedule was reported upwards, finally reaching those responsible for deciding whether to launch or not. This time, the engineers responsible for the construction of the shuttle raised doubts about the safety of launching in the exceptionally cold weather, but that information was distorted on the way to the top management. "This might go wrong" was interpreted as "we have a technical problem, but we can solve it." The reinterpretation occurred in the interface between the spokesman for the engineers and the project management. The latter came to the disastrous conclusion that there was no reason to postpone the launch.

The Commission's report states that, "Safety was inexplicably poorly dealt with given the attention, personnel, and commitment the participants had to the subject."[32] In an attempt to explain the unexplainable, they point to the strong political urge for the launch to come off, putting project management under severe pressure. Budget concerns might have also been involved; several delays had already taxed the resources, which made further delays highly unwanted.

The report further concludes: "There was no system that made it imperative that launch constraints and waivers of launch constraints be considered by all levels

---

[32] *Ibid.*, p. 56.

of management."[33] Therefore, the Commission suggested that the safety system should be distinguished according to that. However, they found no indication that anyone involved in the project had broken any rules; on the contrary, everyone had acted in a way consistent with company standards. This led to the accident being described as "going towards catastrophe by the book."

One can hardly object to the Commission's recommendation to improve the safety system of the space shuttle program. However, one *can* ask why so little attention was given to the fact that the accident could have been avoided by the use of the existing safety system, if it actually had been applied. Whether a system is used or not cannot be attributed to the system, but to the people using it. Thus, tightening the safety regulations is no guarantee for avoiding similar accidents in the future.

Argyris, in his analysis of the Challenger accident, points to two significant circumstances described in the report but not heeded when the Commission gave their recommendations.[34] The first is that the two shuttle project managers who met the concerned engineers face-to-face had differing interpretations of the information they received. One, a deputy shuttle manager with subsidiary responsibility for the project, heard the engineers basically saying delay the launch. The other, higher in rank, perceived it as the engineers raising some questions but not asking for delay. Each could confirm his own view

---

[33] *Ibid.,* p. 104.

[34] In Argyris, C., *ante,* pp. 37–43.

by pointing to selected parts of what had been said during the meeting.

Obviously, they had construed the information differently based on their different roles in the project. The crucial question is: why didn't the two shuttle managers explore their different views with each other, openly acknowledging how their different roles might have influenced their perspectives? If they had done so, they would likely have evolved a clearer picture of the actual situation. Their not doing so might have been due to their being unused to having clarifying discussions between two persons at different levels of the organization. If that is the case—and the Commission's report strongly supports that it is—it is neither the first nor the last time when excessive respect for hierarchy caused disaster.

The other circumstance that Argyris points to is illustrated by the words of a middle manager who tried to get through to his superiors with his concerns about the flawed O-rings. "They were not pleased with my conclusions and my recommendations," he stated when interviewed for the report. Instead of exploring the basis for his concerns, his superiors asked for quantitative data that did not exist and could not possibly be produced in time. By doing so, they were able to stick to their line and, at the same time, have their backs covered if anything went wrong. No one questioned management's uncommunicativeness, or their acting so defensively.

The engineers could not understand why their concerns were rejected. Eventually, they gave it up, "… when it was apparent that I couldn't get anyone to listen."[35] Argyris asks the question: "What would have happened if the engineers had discussed the attributions they were making about their superiors' openness *with* their superiors?"[36] Instead, they fell silent, and their silence was interpreted as agreement with their superiors' decision. Moreover, the management also missed an opportunity to explore what it was about their behavior that caused information and feedback from the rest of the organization not to get across to them.

After the meeting, the engineers concluded that it was up to them to present cast iron proof that launching was risky: "This is in total reverse of what the position usually is in pre-flight conversation or in flight readiness review. It is usually exactly the opposite.[37] *Why didn't the engineers point out that aberrance from standard procedure at the meeting instead of afterwards?* For example, they could have asked the management what information they had that made them take the position they did. In fact, it had been highly unlikely they would raise such a question, since that might be perceived as their questioning management's prerogatives.

The Challenger disaster exemplifies the risk of confusing *communication* with *information logistics*. It is possible to build an information system insuring that data

---

[35] Report of the Presidential Commission: *On the space shuttle Challenger accident, ante,* p. 92.

[36] Argyris, C., *ante,* p. 39.

[37] Report of the Presidential Commission: *On the space shuttle Challenger accident, ante,* p. 93.

is rapidly transferred from one unit of the organization to another, but, often, data is just a small part of the information needed to understand and manage complex operations. In the Challenger example, we are presented with two kinds of worries: the engineers' concern about an accident, and the management's concern about the political—and hereby career—consequences of the project being delayed. These concerns must be gauged against each other to come to a solid conclusion. However, the engineers' concerns were filtered out when passing middle managers who were eager to please their bosses; the political aspects, on the other hand, were highly present in the mind of the managers in charge of the launch. Once again, a better system could not remedy this, but a corporate culture making it possible and desirable to express and discuss intuitive and emotional reactions in addition to hard facts could.

The most serious objection that Argyris raises against the Commission's report is directed to the recommendations to help NASA assure return to safe flight.[38] The analysis part of the report describes extensively how the defensive organizational culture is a decisive factor behind the catastrophe, but that insight is not reflected in the recommendations given. Instead, the report suggests a new oversight group independent of NASA, new job definitions for managers, a new shuttle safety panel, tougher reviews by an audit panel, and a new safety

---

[38] *Ibid.,* pp. 198-201.

position headed by an individual reporting to the direc-
tor.[39] This is an illustrative example of structural solutions
to dynamic problems, a defensive pattern described earlier
in this chapter. Argyris concludes that the members of the
Commission – as most of us – take the defensive routines
for granted, making themselves blind to a crucial aspect
of the reality they have just described. Furthermore, he
indicates, without explicitly saying so, that the measures
described in the recommendations are insufficient to prevent a similar accident in the future. Unfortunately, his
misgivings turned out to be justified.

Columbia, 2003

The similarities between the Challenger disaster of 1986
and the one that destroyed the Columbia space shuttle
13 years later are striking. Once again, a known technical deficiency was the immediate cause of the accident—a piece of foam isolation from the external fuel
tank broke off at launch and struck the left wing of the
shuttle, causing it to collapse when reentering the atmosphere. Once again, the engineers were concerned and
shared this concern with each other, but this time they did
not get through to their superiors at all.

However, the accident report ascribes the technical
deficiencies to a secondary role when explaining what
caused the accident. Just as the committee investigating

---

[39] *Ibid.*, pp. 198-201, summarized in Argyris: *Overcoming organizational
defenses, ante*, p. 42.

the Challenger accident, they pointed out NASA's organizational culture as the primary cause of the disaster:

"Many accident investigations make the same mistake in defining causes. They identify the widget that broke or malfunctioned, then locate the person most closely connected with the technical failure: the engineer who miscalculated an analysis, the operator who missed signals or pulled the wrong switches, the supervisor who failed to listen, or the manager who made bad decisions. When causal chains are limited to technical flaws and individual failures, the ensuing responses aimed at preventing a similar event in the future are equally limited: they aim to fix the technical problem and replace or retrain the individual responsible. Such corrections lead to a misguided and potentially disastrous belief that the underlying problem has been solved (emphasis added). The Board did not want to make these errors. A central piece of our expanded cause model involves NASA as an organizational whole.

In the Board's view, NASA's organizational culture and structure had as much to do with this accident as the External Tank foam. Organizational culture refers to the values, norms, beliefs, and practices that govern how an institution functions. At the most basic level, organizational culture defines the assumptions that employees make as they carry out their work. It is a powerful force that can persist through reorganizations and the reassignment of key personnel.[40]

Further on, the Report specifies the flaws that were found in NASA's organizational culture in general, and its safety culture in particular:

At every juncture of STS-107,[41] the Shuttle Program's structure and processes, and therefore the managers in charge, resisted new information.[42]

The intellectual curiosity and skepticism that a solid safety culture requires was almost entirely absent.[43]

NASA's culture of bureaucratic accountability emphasized chain of command, procedure, following the rules, and going by the book. While rules and procedures were essential for coordination, they had an unintended but negative effect. Allegiance to hierarchy and procedure had replaced deference to NASA engineers' technical expertise.[44]

The organizational structure and hierarchy blocked effective communication of technical problems. Signals were overlooked, people were

---

[40] The Columbia Accident Investigation Board: *Final report, Volume I, August 26, 2003*, p. 177.

[41] Another term for the Columbia Space Shuttle Project

[42] The Columbia Accident Investigation Board: *Final report, ante*, p.181.

[43] *Ibid.*, p.181

[44] *Ibid.*, p.200

silenced, and useful information and dissenting
views did not surface at higher levels.[45]
    … the Board views this cultural resistance as
a fundamental impediment to NASA's effective
organizational performance.[46]

The Investigation Board also paid attention to the Columbia
disaster as "echoing" the one striking Challenger 17 years
earlier. Indeed, the changes suggested by the Presidential
Commission's report on the Challenger accident were
carried through, but they deteriorated gradually through
the years. The report states:

"Cultural norms tend to be fairly resilient.…The
norms bounce back into shape after being stretched
or bent. Beliefs held in common throughout the
organization resist alteration.[47]

This confirms Argyris's doubts about the measures recommended by the Challenger report not being sufficient
to remedy what he saw as the root cause of the accident:
the defensive routines. The norms bounced back because
they were allowed to do so. There was no imperative
in the recommendations compelling the management at

---

[45] *Ibid.,* p.201

[46] *Ibid.,* p.102

[47] Howard E. McCurdy, Inside NASA: *High Technology and Organizational
Change in the U.S. Space Program* (Baltimore: The John Hopkins University
Press, 1993), p. 24; quoted in Report of the Presidential Commission: *On
the space shuttle Challenger accident.* June 5, 1986, p. 101.

NASA to pay attention to norms, regardless of whether they are kept up or not.

However, the history also repeated itself in this respect. Once again, the measures recommended by the Columbia Accident Investigation Board were, without exception, structural, if not to say, bureaucratic. In addition to technical issues, they were about: realistic scheduling of deadlines; joint training for management, safety contingencies, and potential crew members; some changes in the organizational structure; and, finally, a list of routines to be followed.[48] No recommendations were intended to secure that attitudes, behavior, and interaction between those involved in the shuttle program would keep up a sufficient standard to insure crucial information reaching those who needed it. Chain of command being prioritized over knowledge, people being silenced, and alarming signals being ignored can hardly be regarded as structural, or even informational, problems. Instead of asking themselves why the recommendations of the Challenger Commission did not prevent a similar accident from happening, they fell into one of the typical traps thwarting change efforts: doing *more of the same*.[49] Briefly, that means that measures taken are rooted in the same cultural frame of reference as the problems they are intended to solve, thus reinforcing the dysfunctional aspects of the organizational culture instead of changing them. Therefore, there is every reason to be pessimistic

---

[48] *Ibid.*, pp. 226-227.

[49] Watzlawick, P.; Weakland, J.; and Fish, R., *ante,* chapter 3.

about these new recommendations being sufficient to prevent similar accidents in the future. From that perspective, it is a relief that the space shuttle program was closed down in 2011.

As I have already mentioned, the gap between the analysis and the recommendations found in both accident reports is a striking example of finding structural solutions to dynamic problems. It also exemplifies the use of linear logic applied on a non-linear system. The Challenger accident report, and even more the one following the Columbia accident, described discerningly the non-linear dynamics paving the way for the accidents, and when it came to recommending measures to remedy these dynamics, they reverted to linear thinking. It was as if the very idea of "measurement" evoked a simplified picture of the causality behind the accidents. By that, paradoxically, the pregnant and, in other respects, insightful reports ran the risk of reinforcing the problems of NASA's organizational culture instead of the opposite.

Defensive routines of Company X

The organizational dynamics of Company X have many similarities to those described in the space shuttle accident reports. One example is the discussion about the new IT strategy between Jay, the IT manager; John, the marketing manager; and Robert, the production manager.[50]

---

[50] Chapter 3, p. 74.

When Jay was met with opposition from Robert and John, he was at a crossroads. He could persist in criticizing their attitude or he could back off. He chose the latter option by turning the discussion to the least controversial aspect of the move he made—the matter-of-fact issue that was decided on. Probably, there was no deliberate decision behind his doing so; he just gave in to his habitual avoidance of controversies. The other management team members followed the same defensive pattern by not encouraging him to elaborate on his criticism. Instead, they covered up their own defensiveness by using prestigious words like "objectiveness" and "focusing on results." By doing so, they escaped asking themselves several delicate questions: How is it possible to be part of making a decision and, in spite of that, ruin its implementation if you disagree? How loyal are we to each other and to the company? What do our internal power struggles look like, and what consequences do they have for our performance? Who in this team puts company interest ahead of what benefits their own department?

Another example is the way the rest of the team avoided dealing with being uncomfortable with Richard's leadership style.[51] First, they avoided paying attention to it; then they played down the importance of the issue; and, finally they denied it was a problem at all.[52] These

---

[51] Chapter 4, p. 102.

[52] This way of reasoning is known as *"Kettle Logic,"* after a story told in S. Freud's *Jokes and Their Relation to the Unconscious*, in Standard Edition of the *Complete Psychological Works of Sigmund Freud*, trans. A. A. Brill, 13:62 and 206. A man who was accused by his neighbor of having returned a

maneuvers have one single purpose: to avoid putting an unpleasant issue on the agenda.

A third example is the reaction pattern described in Chapter 3 as "he who sees the problem becomes the problem."[53] By punishing the one who raises an unpleasant issue, the team members shift focus from that issue to the behavior of the one person pointing to it. The inclination to matter-of-factness, so characteristic of the management team in other situations, is now conspicuous by its absence, since this time the opposite attitude served defensive purposes better.

It is not far-fetched to assume that defensive routines prevailing in Company X were powerful obstacles to expose and deal with dysfunctional attitudes and behavior, thus thwarting every attempt to change them. The management's habitually clothing these change efforts in bombastic words took away, in the short run, focus from the poor impact they had. In the long run, however, it sapped the employees' respect for their leaders, making it much more difficult for the latter to implement any change whatsoever, even if it was quite uncontroversial. In addition to that, the underlying feeling of downheartedness made it impossible for anyone to mobilize the energy needed to enforce new practices. Of course, the dashing clichés that were served up were insufficient to conquer

---

kettle in a damaged condition offered three arguments to his defense: (1) that he had returned the kettle undamaged; (2) that it was already damaged when he borrowed it; and (3) that he had never borrowed it in the first place.

[53] Chapter 3, p. 56.

the deeper feeling of the change being futile. This feeling of dejection was never openly discussed, and those who resisted change were never compelled to express, or take any responsibility for, their resistance; instead they were allowed to spread discontent without impediment. The final seal of this self-reinforcing calamitous system of actions and feelings was a compensatory cheerfulness, making anyone who brought up problems feel as if he or she was spoiling the party.

This line of reasoning about defensive routines adds a perspective to the team development that the management team of Company X is undergoing at this moment. To be able to deal with the changes necessary to make the company prosper, they must have their eyes opened to the confining dynamic that they, involuntarily, keep up as a team. However, insight into what they are doing isn't enough. They must also mobilize the courage to give each other feedback on defensive maneuvers and other actions detrimental to company success. Furthermore, each one of them has to learn to recognize his or her contribution to the deadlocks of the team dynamics, to be able to take more responsibility for avoiding them.

CHAPTER 6.
DIMENSIONS OF MANAGEMENT TEAM FUNCTIONING

When the management team comes together on the morning of the second day of their offsite, it is with mixed feelings of expectation, anxiety, and seriousness. The shallow cheerfulness that marked the opening of the first day has completely vanished. Jay and Robert exchange jesting comments, but these do not diminish the impression of a group of people approaching their undertaking seriously. This is confirmed by the others smiling at their jokes, but no one is trying to engage with them in order to avoid more serious matters.

When they are all seated, one of the consultants invites them to reflect on thoughts and feelings about yesterday's events, and also to share dreams of the night if they want to and can remember any. Robert chuckles, catching the attention of the others: "I had a dream. I don't think it has anything to do with what we did yesterday, but it was rather funny." Encouraged by the rest of the team, he continues: I dreamt that I was working at a circus, and I had a hell of a job keeping the lions from escaping from their cages. Every time I'd get all of them behind bars, there was a midget who would open the cage, and then I'd have to start chasing them back in again. Then, suddenly the scene changed and I was on a savannah in Africa, where I was riding on a big lion in the middle of a large pride."

The others engage vividly in suggesting interpretations of Robert's dream. Eventually, one of the consultants asks Robert: "What do you think this dream means to you?" At first, he dodges the question by laughing it off, then he says: "Well, I think we're letting the genie out of the lamp here. I mean, we're letting out things that have been unpleasant to talk about. Perhaps I'm trying to withstand it, but at the same time…it is as if I both want and don't want it to happen."

The others nod in the affirmative. Victor says, "I know that feeling of both wanting and not wanting. It's like when I made my first parachute jump. If the instructor hadn't pushed me, I'd still be clinging to that plane door." Jane points out that Robert actually lets the lions out on the savannah in the end of the dream, and that he seems very satisfied with having done that. Mary chimes in, saying that it is precisely for that purpose they have come to this offsite, to let all kinds of beasts out of their cages. Jane shivers, saying, "That doesn't sound very pleasant," and everyone falls silent, as if they have been reminded of the seriousness of their present task.

It is Jay who breaks the silence: "I've been thinking a lot about yesterday. It felt sort of okay, but I don't think we pushed the issues far enough." Asked about what issues he has in mind, he answers that it is chiefly the one he himself brought up, about Robert and John obstructing his ambition to make the IT department more influential. "It felt good to bring it up, but I have a strong feeling that I didn't get anywhere. I mean, it could happen again. I heard nothing from Robert and John that made me believe they won't screw me again." One of the consultants asks, "What do you want to do about that?" Jay looks confused; apparently, he had not expected the question. After a while, he replies, "I want them to assure me that it won't happen again, and that they will speak directly to me if they meet any sour reactions from their people." The consultant exhorts him to address Robert and John directly, and he does so.

At first, they try to reject Jay's version of what happened during the discussion, but, first the consultants and then several of the other team members object to their doing so. When they realize that weaseling out will take them nowhere, Robert and John swear they had no intention to steamroll Jay, or to make things more difficult for the IT people. However, their way of saying it reveals no signs of remorse or consideration. When asked if they really mean they are sorry, they both affirm being so, presenting faces of wounded innocence. Determined not to let them off the hook, the consultant asks the other team members how trustworthy they find Robert and John's answers. The question makes them squirm, but, after a while, Susan says, "It didn't sound very convincing." Mary agrees. Richard declares he has to assume they mean what they say. One of the consultants says that his statement sounds more wishful than convinced, and Richard concedes that it might be so. The consultant goes on by pointing to the manipulative quality of Robert and John's behavior, and to the others' letting it pass without objection, in spite of not believing them. John starts defending his behavior, but is interrupted by Mary, who says, "You are defending yourself instead of listening to what we are trying to say." Robert agrees that John is getting defensive and admits that there is some truth in the feedback they are getting. He recalls a time when he was in a situation similar to the one Jay brought up, and he had felt about the same way.

Robert's admission causes the intensity of the criticism from the others to decrease, making room for a more investigative and conversational tone to arise. This makes John less defensive and, after a while, he can also admit that his response to Jay's request was, in reality, an attempt to protect himself for the moment. He also admits that he isn't more inclined now than he was before to allow the IT department to have influence over his turf. This time it is Jane who reacts: "So you deliberately don't give a shit about what we have decided together?" John defends himself against the accusation, but several of the others understand his remark in a similar way, and he soon finds himself backed into a corner. Finally, he snaps. "Why should I follow every stupid decision we make in this bunch? No one else does." Then he gets on his feet, looking as if he is about to leave the room, and confines himself to walking around within it. The others look at him but say nothing. Finally, Mary tells him to "sit down." John hesitates a moment, then follows her request.

With assistance from the consultants, Jay, Susan, and Mary give John feedback on his behavior, and on how it affects them. John eventually calms down and lowers his guard. He listens to the others and stops himself when he is about to raise objections to what they are saying. When they are done, he says, "I hear you. I know I have a short fuse.

Sometimes I can't stand those long discussions leading nowhere, but I promise I'll get better at listening to you."

Mary answers, smiling: "Sounds okay to me." Obviously, she is still having doubts about John's sincerity, but she chooses to respond to him in a positive way. The others choose to do the same, probably relieved by having the most oppositional team member now, at least, showing some good will. Jay makes an attempt to redirect the discussion to the betrayal he felt he had been subjected to, but nobody is interested in picking up that thread again.

The silence that follows is broken by Richard, who starts to describe how he has been ruminating on his leadership, and whether he has expressed his goals for the team and the company as clearly as he thought he had. He sympathizes with John feeling restless. "It is like watching myself when I was 20 years younger, but, as the years have gone by, I've learned to curb that side of myself, partly to make room for others' opinions, and partly because I could see how people were dodging me. Maybe I'm less good at keeping my impatience in check than I thought." Jane makes an attempt to counter Richard's self-criticism, but stops when she realizes that no one believes what she is saying, not even she herself. The others say nothing, but their facial expressions reveal that they recognize Richard in his description of himself, and they appreciate him putting it into words. They are obviously relieved that Richard has acknowledged the feedback they have given him.

After that, Jane, Mary, and Victor share their reflections on yesterday's events. Jane has thought a lot about the role she's having in the team. She shared that she often finds herself in a position of trying to calm the situation down by mediating between the others. They confirm that she does this often, and they encourage her to express her own opinion more distinctly. If not, they suggest, she runs the risk of being neglected by them.

Mary reports that she was too inactive the day before, and that she will not allow herself to continue to be so today. Victor catches onto her statement, saying that he feels the same way. When he is asked to express that in his own words, he describes how he tries not to get involved in the power struggles during their team meetings back home. He wants to be respected for his competence and his experience, but he often feels he is being left out, especially when the discussions get heated. Mary asks him if he withdraws from the power struggles because he wants to, or because he sees himself coming out short from them, and he answers, evasively, "both, I think." The others persist, determined not to let themselves be brushed aside by his defensive remark, and he eventually admits he wants to fight more for his points of view in the management team, but he isn't sure that he would have any success if he tried to do that. In his view, other team members are better at doing that. Asked whom he is referring to by that remark, he points to John, Richard, Robert, and Mark.

The consultants try different approaches to helping Victor scrutinize the ways he blocks himself from entering the stage to compete with other team members for attention. He dodges the challenge, showing clearly that he thinks he has already taken up too much of the team's time. The consultants drop the issue, firmly determined to pick it up again when the team's process has advanced to a deeper level.

During all this time, Mark has kept a low profile, as he did for most of the day before, and now he can sense the other team members' glances are looking in his direction. Hurriedly, he therefore proclaims that he got a lot out of yesterday's events, especially the openness shown by several of the others. Asked to specify, he singles out Richard and Robert. Everyone looks surprised, and Jay asks: "Why those two?" Mark explains that he can see how Richard is struggling to get through with his idea about how he wants the management team to work, and that he has the courage to show his feelings. When it comes to Robert, he becomes vaguer: "It's nothing I can point to, it's more of a feeling." He adds that Jay has also shown a lot of himself, but this causes Jay to look more bewildered than complimented. Observing this reaction, and the skeptical looks from the rest of the team, one of the consultants points out to Mark that he is not seen as trustworthy by the other team members. Before Mark has a chance to respond to that, Mary says it seems as if he is pointing to the persons he wants to get in good with rather than talking about what he actually feels. Mark tries to defend himself by elaborating why he picked Richard and Robert, but that only increases the skepticism around him. He falls silent, obviously getting nowhere with his defense, and the others continue to focus their attention on him. Eventually, he tells them he has had a rough time since his father died a month ago, which is causing him to ponder a lot about what is important in life. The faces around him change from skepticism to seriousness and compassion while he is talking, but no one says anything. Eventually, Richard clears his throat and says he has had similar thoughts, to which Jane nods her agreement. The conversation ceases again, and, after a moment of reflection, the silence is broken by one of the consultants asking Mark if he wants to say something more. He answers that he could speak about this for hours, but he feels it is enough for the moment.

Finally, all team members, except Susan, have shared their reflections on the team process so far. She doesn't show any inclination to speak up, so one of the consultants addresses her directly: "You haven't said anything." She answers that she didn't sleep a wink last night, and she makes a point of saying that had nothing to do with what went on the day before; she always sleeps badly when she is away from home. The consultant tries again: "But, if it would have been something about yesterday's course of events that, after all, disturbed your sleep, what might it have been then?" Susan hesitates a moment before she decides not to swallow the bait. The other team members say nothing, so the issue is dropped.

Whenever the participants of a team process like this one have time for individual reflection, there is an important part of learning going on. The emotional strain built up by the unsolved tensions between team members activates their psychological defense mechanisms, which, consequently, causes them to fend off feedback from each other, as well as any disturbing thoughts of their own. When the strain is reduced, the defenses will diminish, opening the team up to processing what has been repressed. This happens especially during their nights of sleep.

In general, the process of dream-work can be seen as a means to integrate experiences of the day with our conception of ourselves, and with our picture of the world around us. This process of integration operates mainly beyond reach of the conscious mind. However, during a development program like the one described here, dream content is a source of metaphors of a development that might otherwise be difficult to put into words. This is one reason behind the consultants' inviting the team members to pay attention to their dreams during the reflection round. The other reason is a wish on their part to challenge the rationalistic and matter-of-fact oriented notion of reality that is predominating within the team, and to open them up for other sources of information.

In addition to this, a reflection round, in which everyone is expected to share thoughts and feelings, has one more function. During the ordinary process work, the principle is that he or she who wants to say something has to take an initiative to do so. Nothing in this way of conducting team training insures the members any airtime to speak. The reason for this is simple: that is how it is in real life, *i.e.,* during the days at Company X. No consultants walk around there insuring that people get heard. Everyone has to rely on his own power of initiative, and on his courage, to say what he feels has to be said.

Of course, it is easy to create some structure, or schedule, distributing the time more equally between the team members at the offsite. This could be argued for, since one hallmark of a well-functioning team is that everyone on the team talks and listens in roughly equal measure. While the structure would facilitate team communication during the offsite, it would likely not continue to do so when they return to their workaday lives. Rather, the short-term gain in smoother interaction would soon be overrun by the long-term effect from deflating frustration as a fuel for change. On the other hand, to be neglected repeatedly because one does not have the guts to speak one's mind is to propel change far more efficiently than being invited to a protected scene created by someone else.[54]

However, the drawback of this Darwinian principle is that it can enforce the prevailing distribution of power and airtime for the team. Low-status members get used to holding back their points of view, and the others get used to looking at them as not being talkative. Since willingness to speak is poorly correlated to having something bright or innovative to say, the team will be deprived of the wisdom of the non-talkers. The joint reflections at the early stages of the team development program give those members a chance to show that they have a potential to contribute to the teamwork that does not show otherwise. In the long run, increased attention to each other, and the expectation that, in the matter of course everyone will take an active part, brings the competence of all the team members to light.

The team has now reached the stage when the members are starting to look more critically at each other's statements and actions, and they are also putting that criticism into words. Still, they need support from the consultants

---

[54] This, in my opinion, is a key to understanding why leadership and team training in general give such poor results.

to do this instead of giving feedback spontaneously—
nevertheless, this is a great step forward in comparison
to how the team acted just one day earlier. What is new
is that they have an increased attention to, and awareness
of, each other, and that the emerging openness shown by
several of them has led to a growing mutual trust. This
makes it possible, and desirable, for them to hold each
other accountable for their contributions to the team's
success, which, as we have seen in chapter 4, is one of Jon
Katzenbach's criteria for a real management team. The
most significant example of this is when Jane nails John
for ignoring the decision made by the team in the meeting
before last. The fact that the others are catching on to the
criticism indicates that the team is about to incorporate
corrective and demanding feedback into its repertory.

Another important sign of the team having taken steps
forward is that the feedback increasingly addresses what
is happening in the actual moment. Jane's reaction to
John's behavior illustrates that as well. A "here-and-now"
feedback is far more effective than one addressing something that happened earlier. There are many reasons for
this. The recollection of an episode is usually distorted
by self-justification, which often leads to disputes over
what really happened. Moreover, the emotions evoked in
the situation might be difficult to revive when they have
died away, leading to an intellectualized discussion over
something that is basically emotional. In addition to that,
the feelings of the receiver of the feedback might be reinforced with indignation over the sender having not given

the feedback when it was fresh. Finally, and, perhaps, the strongest reason: all change occurs in the present. What is done is done, and promising that it will not happen again certainly has some symbolic importance, but it is no guarantee of a behavioral change. Acting differently here and now is a far more reliable token of real change than promises about improved behavior in the future.

John is the one of the team members who has resisted the ongoing development process most conspicuously. He was against the approach from the beginning, and he has done little since then to conceal his dislike of what the team has been going through. Those making serious contributions to the development process have every reason to be annoyed at his disparaging and, at times, quite aggressive obstruction of the process. From a superficial point of view, he might be seen as an impediment to team progress. An appropriate measure, based on this shallow perspective, would have been to dismiss him from the team, giving the others a chance to develop without disturbances. However, a deeper analysis of the situation gives several arguments for that not being a good idea.

First, John's restlessness is also vitalizing the team's group dynamics. Without him, they would run the risk of falling into a comfortable but stagnant consensus mode, i.e., adapting themselves to a "conspiracy of decency," prioritizing peace and quiet above intensity and confrontation. This aspiration for calm and unanimity is counterproductive for the development of team dynamics, as well as for team performance. John's behavior might be seen as a problem for the other team members, but not for the team development process. To see it from only the perspective of the team members would be to apply a simplistic and linear perspective on change dynamics. It is not the "no" men or "no" women who stall the process; it is those who say neither yes nor no.

Second, the fact that John is explicit in his resistance does not mean that he is the only one acting as a check on the development process. It is an easy way out for the other team members — deliberately or unconsciously — to let him represent misgivings that all of them can have at times. By projecting[55] doubts of their own onto John, the others will appear more apt to change than they really are. If John were to leave the team, the others might be compelled to acknowledge their own resistance to change, but they might also pick out another team member to fill the role of scapegoat. This would be detrimental to the dawning openness and trust in the team.

The fact that John is the target for projections from the other team members does not relieve him from responsibility for his behavior. The feedback given to him from the others is mostly uncontaminated, *i.e.,* it is an expression of how the others perceive him rather than of what they have projected onto him. His reluctance about self-reflection makes him particularly dependent on distinct feedback from people around him if he is to get a perspective on his behavior. There are also clear signs of him letting the feedback sink in, and trying to act constructively on

---

[55] The defense mechanism Projection is described in the Appendix, p. 292.

it, even though he is not willing to meet Jay's request for redress. The other team members let him get away with that, mainly because the team process has not reached the stage when it will be possible to deal with power struggles. The difficulties of addressing these issues has to do with each of the team members having been aggrieved by being steamrolled, manipulated, or rebuked by the others. Since being aggrieved is often associated with being weak, they will not be expected to approach these problems until there is a solid base of trust within the team. Indeed, Jay has put the issue on the agenda, but, as we saw in chapter 3, he has only done so in a way that makes it easy for the others to dodge it.

Mark's stepping in, and the reactions to his doing so, are interesting in many ways. So far, he has succeeded in keeping a low profile, distinguishing himself neither positively nor negatively. His behavior is hinting at what will, later, become obvious: he tries to avoid getting into the focus of the others' attention and, thereby, being compelled to show more of himself than he is willing to reveal. The reason for his reluctance to open up might be found in his personality, but he can also have attitudes and behaviors that will not bear the light of day. Indications of the latter became clear to the consultants when they interviewed the team members before the offsite. Many of them hinted that they had difficulties in cooperating with Mark's department, even though no one pointed directly at him as being the problem. On direct questions from the consultants, several of them reported that it was common knowledge within the company that Mark performed below par, but no one said that to him directly, nor had it been brought up in the management team. Until now, Mark has been protected by the defensive routines of Company X, but he has every reason to fear that he will not be protected for much longer.

From this perspective, Mark's behavior can be regarded as a tactical approach to the feedback given to him. Mary's remark that he sucks up to those whom he wants to get in good with is very much to the point, and his reaction of getting even more defensive corroborates that. Still unsuccessful in warding the others off, he plays the card of his deceased father. At this stage of the team's development, team members are not able to see through the manipulation of his using a profoundly personal experience to immunize himself against corrective feedback, or, to be more precise, they are not able to do so consciously. Intuitively, they react by becoming silent instead of catching on to a theme that everyone can relate to. The deadlock arises because team members have to deal with two contradictory images: one of a person showing sincerity by being personal, and another, of the same person being tactical and defensive. What Mark really displays is a kind of "as-if openness," which is aimed at concealing rather than disclosing. In contrast to real openness, which nurtures trust, this kind of personal revelation leads to the opposite of that outcome when it is used defensively.

This episode also illustrates how behavior is perceived differently at different levels of openness and trust. At a more superficial level, Mark's statement would probably be received as a manifestation of openness and honesty. At a more profound level, he would probably get feedback on the manipulative use of a touching narrative. In the intermediate phase—which is where the team is at the moment—the members can sense that Mark is playing a tactical game, but the level of openness and trust is not sufficient for anyone to bring that feeling into the light. As will be shown in the next part, the Level of Openness and Trust is a fundamental dimension of team functioning, one that is crucial for the understanding of team dynamics and team performance.

The level of openness and trust (LOT)

Most people would probably agree that *openness* is a valuable asset to any team aiming to achieve something of importance. A free flow of facts, ideas, and opinions, unrestrained by fear, tactics, and tactfulness, will make teamwork go faster and smoother. The quality of the result of the work is also very likely to be better, since it is based on a wide variety of experience and knowledge. This is especially true for teams dependent on efficient information processing for their success, as is the case with management teams. Consequently, an important task for a management team is to secure a level of openness that is sufficient to keep the decision and implementation processes running smoothly.

It is also reasonable to assume that *trust* is a prerequisite for openness; people who trust each other share information, beliefs, and confidences that they would probably withhold if they were surrounded by people they do not trust. By increasing trust, we can expect that openness will increase as well. In terms of cause-and-effect, we might say that trust *causes* openness.

But how can we increase trust? Obviously, we cannot just decide to trust each other. Nor can we push ourselves to trust other people. Trust is something that grows or diminishes as a consequence of how people act toward each other. So, the key question is: What behavior evokes trust?

My suggested answer to that question is: openness evokes trust. People putting their cards on the table, giving no indications of manipulation, calculation, defensiveness, or hidden motives, gain our trust. What you see is what you get; no backstabbing or other unpleasant surprises are to be expected. No need to watch one's step. It feels safe to return such openness by being open, too.

The mutual dependence of openness and trust, then, constitutes a kind of circular movement. Openness is a prerequisite for trust, and trust is a prerequisite for openness (see diagram 2).

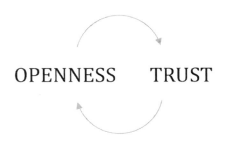

OPENNESS   TRUST

Diagram 2. The Relationship Between Openness and Trust

We recognize this circular causality, or paradox, from *the Prisoners' Dilemma*, described earlier.[56] *The paradox of openness and trust* can be formulated this way: I want to be open to you, but first I have to trust you, so you must be open first. You are reasoning the same way, so we end up waiting for each other to take the first step. We are deadlocked in a vicious circle, consolidating the actual level of openness and trust, but preventing ourselves from coming any closer. In order to grow our relationship, we have to transcend the paradox and break out of the closed circle in which we are trapped.

Transcending the paradox of openness and trust: The LOT helix™

Imagine a group of people meeting for the first time. They have not yet had any opportunity to be open, or to build

---

[56] Chapter 5 p. 136.

mutual trust; they are starting off at a zero level, or, in terms of relational depth, at a surface level.

At this point, building openness and trust is easy. Someone says "Hi," and looks friendly; another person responds with a smile, adding a comment on something uncontroversial; a third person joins the talk, also in a positive manner. Soon, everyone in the group has joined in. Openness furthers trust, and trust furthers openness, which furthers more openness, and so on. Instead of running idle at the same level, the circle bores deeper and deeper, turning the circle in Diagram 2 into a helix (see Diagram 3):

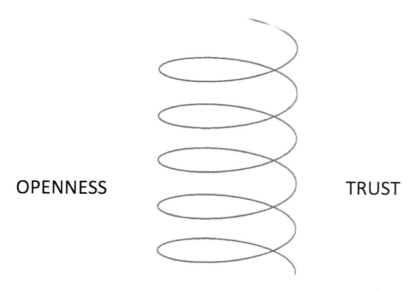

OPENNESS   TRUST

Diagram 3. The Level of Openness and Trust (LOT) Helix

This spontaneous group formation can be described as a step-by-step trial and error process. One person says something; another answers, and the others nod, laugh, look uncomfortable, or ignore what was said. The members of the group are sensitive to how their words and behavior are perceived by the others. More or less subtle signs of disapproval lead to adjustments and self-censorship. Together, step-by-step, they build the space and restrictions that constitute the emerging group norm. This norm is a mainly subconscious, but very powerful, regulator of what the group members feel free to say and do. The level of openness, *i.e.*, how much of themselves they dare to show, is adjusted to accord with how open the others are. The less the others conceal what they really think, the more a team member can trust she will be accepted when showing herself.

The spiral movement corresponds to a deepening of the interpersonal relations.[57] In addition to increasing openness and trust, it is also correlated to important qualities of human interaction: awareness of others and of oneself, interpersonal closeness, intellectual and emotional vitality, and a sense of meaning and fulfillment. All these phenomena are basically emotional, which makes it difficult, not to say impossible, to gauge the level of openness and trust with any scientific precision. Nevertheless, to the members of a group, it is a highly palpable reality. As will be shown in the next section, it also has a strong explanatory value in assessing a team's capacity for efficient action.

---

[57] This is the reason for it being drawn downwards, which usually annoys sales people, since, in their world, being good is tantamount to going up. However, in this context, I prefer the metaphorical connection to growing deeper relations.

However, this spiral movement does not go on forever, even though it is theoretically possible for it to do so. All groups have a tendency to level off at what they feel is a comfortable and non-threatening point. I use the name, the Level of Social Convenience (SOC-level) for this refuge on the path of group formation (see Diagram 4).

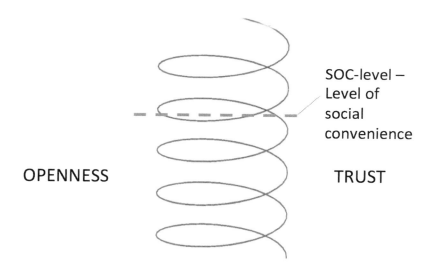

SOC-level –
Level of
social
convenience

OPENNESS

TRUST

Diagram 4. The Level of Social Convenience (SOC-level)

At this level, the group members have gotten to know each other, and they have become as close as possible without having to address tensions or conflicts between them. The emotional exchange is kept on a level that makes it possible for everyone to have control of what they themselves are revealing to the others. The conversational tone is mainly pleasant, supportive, and conciliatory. Discussions are confined to topics that are fairly uncontroversial. The unspoken code of conduct is: Say and do what keeps up the good atmosphere, and avoid everything that anyone might take offense at. This is very similar to the attitude that Chris Argyris has named *skilled incompetence* (Chapter 5, p. 133).

There is no mystery as to why the deepening of the group process halts at the SOC-level. The assumed risk of going further, toward more openness, increases when the harmless revelations have been shared, making it harder to comment on the behavior of the others, or exposing new aspects of oneself without touching on sensitive issues. The potential sources of irritation and conflict will make themselves felt, but the group climate does not allow them to surface. Instead, the group members continue to limit their attention to the uncontroversial aspects of being together.

Every group finds its SOC-level, but the depth of this level differs largely between groups. How close people are getting spontaneously depends mainly on the distribution of personalities in the group, and also on its purpose. A group meeting to discuss existential philosophy is probably comfortable with more personal openness than one gathering to play soccer. Moreover, it also depends on the gravity of the potential conflicts anticipated by group members. If they have reason to believe there are fundamental disagreements between them, the building of openness and trust will probably halt at a more superficial level than otherwise. The Level of Social Convenience implies having a safe margin to anything that might make being together unpleasant.

Groups that have attained the Level of Social Convenience often describe themselves as "tight" and "outspoken." However, these characteristics are usually more wishful than accurate, and that will show if the group is subjected to inner or outer pressure. The "outspokenness" on this level is based on the premise that no one will speak out if doing so would ruin the good atmosphere. This makes the "tightness" an illusion, since the group, due to lack of experience of dealing with difficult issues, would probably scatter if really put to the test.

A team might escape dealing with emotional unpleasantness, but that does not insure a satisfactory team performance. Maintaining the pleasant atmosphere is usually done at the expense of efficiency, even though the opposite is often assumed. Anyone taking full responsibility for using his or her competence and influential capability will probably be seen as the one causing rivalry in the team. Since this will inevitably stir issues of power and influence that might lead to conflicts, the members of a SOC-level team will keep a low profile compared to their actual capacity. This paves the way for mediocre performance.

Thus, dealing with complicated and challenging tasks demands a level of openness and trust that is deeper than one that is sufficient to make people feel comfortable. The more complex or emotionally demanding tasks, the more openness and trust are needed to handle them efficiently. A team of workers at the conveyor belt can perform adequately without having to deepen their interpersonal relations, at least if they have someone who tells them what to do. However, if they were given a joint responsibility for coordinating the assembly, they would have to pay much more attention to the interaction of the team. It would, therefore, be necessary to deal with contradictory aspirations and needs, as well as differences in working abilities and willingness to work. Interpersonal conflicts would have to be resolved before they interfere with the work process, or block it entirely. Everyone would have to contribute to finding the best solutions to upcoming problems. Sharing responsibility is far more demanding in terms of depth of process than just having to answer for each one's own stage in the operation.

Teams shouldering an expanded responsibility sometimes undergo *team-building,* to prepare them for the new challenges. The idea is that they, by doing things together, will learn to accept their differences in personality, which will make their cooperation smoother. Unfortunately, there is seldom any explicit idea of how deep and close the interaction has to be for the team to be able to tackle its most difficult tasks. Instead, there is a vague, general notion that people will work better together if they share exciting experiences, like mountain climbing or white-water rafting. Adding features like discussing and committing themselves to goals, distribution of roles, ways of working, and code of conduct makes the team-building more useful, but these will have little impact on the dynamics of the team. As we have seen in the example of the management team committing themselves to a code of conduct (Chapter 5, p. 143), agreements about behavior and conduct are no guarantee that people will act in accordance with these agreements, even if they unanimously entered into them. The level of openness and trust, and other characteristics of the team's dynamics, will have far more influence on actual behavior.

Still, the concept of Level of Openness and Trust makes it possible to formulate a precise goal for team-building: *to insure a level of openness and trust that is sufficient for the team to carry out its most demanding tasks.* I will call this level Sufficient Level of Openness and Trust (Suf-LOT), as shown in Diagram 5.

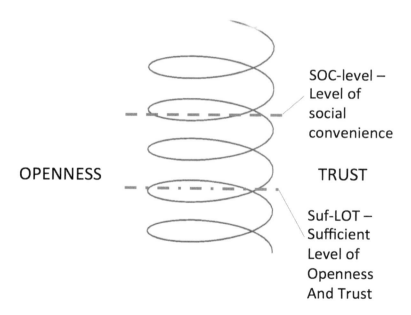

OPENNESS   TRUST

SOC-level –
Level of
social
convenience

Suf-LOT –
Sufficient
Level of
Openness
And Trust

Diagram 5. Sufficient Level of Openness and Trust (Suf-LOT)

This leads to the question of how one is to know if a working team, project team, or a management team, has attained a sufficient level of openness and trust. Finding objective and measurable criteria is difficult, if not impossible. However, teams that operate on a too-superficial level have several characteristics in common: the interpersonal dynamics lack energy and vitality; communication is formal and shallow; dissatisfaction is expressed in action—or lack of action—instead of in words, or is expressed in situations where no one is obliged to do anything about the cause of the dissatisfaction. Feedback is kept to oneself, even when team members are obviously reacting to the behaviors of each member; suggestions are ignored; and failure is explained away or blamed on someone outside the team.

Naturally, these deficiencies of team dynamics are detrimental for the team's ability to fulfill its assignments. When facing a task more complex than the team, as a system, is capable of handling at the existent level of openness and trust, they are predestined to fail. Since managing complexity depends on having access to creativity and spontaneity, and on not being afraid of looking bad, as discussed earlier (Chapter 3, p. 57), lack of trust will prove to be a considerable impediment to excellent performance. A team that is unable to deal with complexity has no other option than to use measures based on a simplified notion of reality. Eventually, even these attempts to solve the team's problems will turn wan, since, intuitively, everyone expects them to fail. However, the unsolved core problem, which is undiscussable and unsolvable, will certainly generate symptoms in different parts of the organization (see Diagram 6); because these secondary problems are more tangible and less sensitive, the team will address them instead. For example, infighting between the marketing manager and the manager of sales might be too unpleasant for the team to deal with. However, if their unsolved affairs cause a conflict between a sales person and a marketing man—as they probably do—the management team might spend hours discussing measurements to improve cooperation at the subordinate level, carefully dodging their internal conflict. The root conflict being unsolved paves the way for more symptoms and symptom treatments, solving the issues of the moment but not of the long run. Problems supposedly solved turn up on the agenda again and again. "I thought that we solved this half a year ago; why is it coming up again?" is a common comment in teams that are incapable of addressing their root problems.

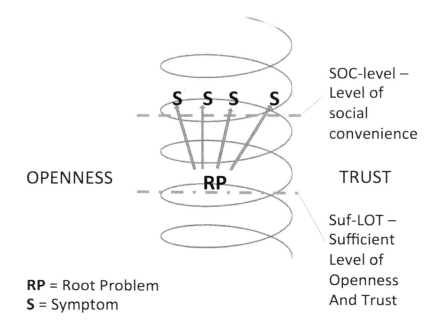

OPENNESS

RP = Root Problem
S = Symptom

SOC-level –
Level of
social
convenience

TRUST

Suf-LOT –
Sufficient
Level of
Openness
And Trust

Diagram 6. Root Problem vs. Symptom Treatment at the
Social Convenience Level

The processing capability that comes with deeper levels of openness and trust can be compared metaphorically to a computer processor. My first computer had a clock speed of 8 MHz and a RAM memory of 512 KB. It worked well with simple word processor and spreadsheet programs, but if I were to try to run even the simplest version of Word for Windows, the system would collapse immediately. Soon, I quit trying to use complex programs and, instead, stuck to those I knew my computer could handle. Similarly, a team with a too-superficial level of openness and trust are compelled to drop complex and emotionally challenging issues and give their time to simpler ones. If they, all the same, try to do the former, the team, as a system, will slow down, the work will be dull and uninspired, and, eventually, it will grind to a halt.[58]

The members of a team operating at a too-superficial level of openness and trust are seldom aware that their inefficiency can be traced to their way of relating to each other. A company, or an organization of any kind, affords many circumstances on which failure can be blamed: lazy coworkers, computer problems, stupid customers, state of the market, bad luck, etc. This "culture of excuses" is reinforced by another typical characteristic of a team on a too-shallow level: *reluctance to hold each other accountable for inadequate performance and behavior*. For a team to be able to maintain high quality, it is necessary that everyone shoulder responsibility, not only for his or her behavior, but also for correcting other team members when they act contrarily to the team's and company's good. In a dysfunctional team, this self-adjusting feedback function is replaced by a kind of a cronyism: I don't bring your faults to light, and you don't bring mine. When this pattern is established, often disguised as "mutual respect," the team has lost its ability to better their performance without resolute help from the outside.

Obviously, an inadequate team level of openness and trust will also have consequences for individual team

---

[58] The LOT also explains the dynamic behind the well-known *Parkinson's Law of Triviality,* or the *Bike-shed Effect:* discussing the location of an atomic reactor is done in 20 minutes, after which the team spends three hours discussing the best place for a bike-shed. The reason is, according to Parkinson, that the average person cannot understand the implications of the first issue, but everyone understands what a bike-shed is. Parkinson, *ante,* pp 29-30.

members. The lack of distinct feedback, verbal or non-verbal, will not only deprive the members of possibilities to grow and learn, it will also nurture a feeling of insignificance, if not completely so, then, at least, as compared to one's potential. This feeling is bolstered by a sense of not obtaining a firm grip on the reality that the team is supposed to handle. Resignation, and even cynicism, are easily grown in a group climate like this.

The level of openness and trust vs. management team duties

The LOT helix applies to all kind of groups, but it is especially important for the understanding of management team performance. This is mainly because the quality and outcome of management teamwork has vast consequences for many people. It is especially true for top management teams, because of their having an overall strategic responsibility, not only for making the right decisions, but also for setting a culture that supports company success. The way top management team members act, internally as well as directed outwardly, sets norms and standards for the whole organization.

In this section, we are going to relate the level of openness and trust to two other dimensions of management team function: *level of task complexity* and *level of cooperation*. The descriptions of these are mainly taken from research made by the Swedish economist Bo Mattsson.[59] We will also relate these dimensions to Jon Katzenbach's distinction, *single leader team vs. a real management team*, mentioned in Chapter 4, p. 118.

Mattsson groups management team tasks into three categories:

- *Operational tasks:* low degree of uncertainty, short time span;
- *Complex tactical tasks:* medium degree of uncertainty, medium time span; and
- *Strategic and developmental tasks:* high degree of uncertainty, long time span.

These categories represent a scale from simplicity to complexity. Usually, the *operational tasks* — what to do, and who is to do it — can easily be decided by referring to how similar issues have been dealt with in the past. The person in charge for implementing an operational decision usually has firm control over the resources needed.

However, the situation is quite the opposite when it comes to *strategic and development tasks*. The decision basis there is complex and often full of contradictions. The degree of uncertainty makes it difficult to predict how team members and their departments will be affected by alternative decisions. Information about what is wise

---

to do is continuously coming up, often in the interface between departments, or between the organization and the world around it. To a large extent, the work is performed across departments, which means that no single manager has control over all the requirements for coming to the best solutions.

Complex tactical tasks fall between operational and strategic tasks. The level of uncertainty is higher than in operational tasks, but rarely as high as in strategic ones. One or two departments might be involved, sometimes compelling two department managers to find a solution together.

An increased task complexity calls for closer cooperation between team members. Mattsson identifies three levels of cooperation:

- *Information exchange*: Team members present their issues to inform each other. The discussions are matter-of-fact; personal engagement is limited.
- *Cooperation*: Team members inform each other when it is necessary for solving a problem that has arisen. Disputes are solved through negotiation.
- *Close collaboration*: Crucial issues are thoroughly discussed. Disputes are solved through an exploratory dialog, aiming at attaining common understanding of the different points of view. Conflicts are scrutinized, emotions are openly expressed, and personal relations are regarded as an important

aspect of working together. Personal engagement is of a high grade.[60]

Openness, trust, closeness, and commitment—qualities associated with the LOT helix described above—are important determinants of the team's ability to work together. Thus, the difference between the three levels of cooperation can be expressed as: *Working in a spirit of close collaboration demands a deeper Level of Openness and Trust than dealing with specific issues, and even more when compared to a level sufficient for sharing information.*

Finally, Mattsson brings complexity of tasks and level of cooperation together into the following synthesis, expressed as four "types" of management teams. The types represent four different states; hypothetically, the same team can alternate between them:

- Information team
- Sounding-board team
- Problem-solving team
- Holistic-integrative team.[61]

The most important function of an *information team* is, not surprisingly, to secure an information exchange among its members. This, as when dealing with operational issues,

---

[60] *Ibid.,* pp. 61-62.

[61] *Ibid.,* pp. 202–210.

is a comparatively simple task. Indeed, all team members must commit themselves to it, but it does not take a high level of intellectual or emotional involvement to participate in the discussion. It is acceptable to lean back when one's own department is not directly affected by the information. Since problems addressed at this level usually have an answer or a solution that is "right," members who do not have expertise or first-hand information about the topic discussed might as well stay out of the discussion.

The *sounding-board team* is a forum for its members to raise issues and get input from the others. It also offers the members an opportunity to get comments on leadership dilemmas with which they may be struggling. The variety of possible solutions to complex problems makes invaluable the feedback from discerning and committed teammates representing different perspectives. However, sagacity and commitment is not enough. Since coming to a decision is essentially an emotional process,[62] the team members must also feel free to contribute with emotional and intuitive responses. Consequently, the sounding-board team implies a deeper level of openness and trust than the information team. The team member raising an issue must be able to trust the others will not use the information he reveals, or the fact that he is asking for help, to better their own odds in the internal struggle for power. It is far too easy to be clever at a colleague's expense, thereby strengthening one's own position, and,

---

[62] This is convincingly proved in Damasio, A., *Descartes' Error: Emotion, Reason and the Human Brain* (New York: Putnam Books, 1994).

at the same time, hiding this intention behind an apparent "helpfulness." If this is going on without anyone calling attention to it, the team's function as a sounding-board will turn into a sham or cease to exist as a feature on the agenda.

The *problem-solving team* engages in discussing problems of a single department, multiple departments, or of the company as a whole. This form is suitable for semi-complex short- or medium-term issues, *i.e.,* production disturbances affecting more than one department, or personnel matters of principle. Everything said about the sounding-board team, above, in terms of commitment and trust, is also valid for the problem-solving team. In addition, it is even more important for sounding-board team members to put their own interests aside in favor of what is beneficial for the company as a whole. Two consequences of a sufficient level of openness and trust are decisive here: (1) the heightened awareness of manipulations and hidden agendas, which will distort the discussion; and (2) the courage to call attention to anyone using them.

The *holistic-integrative team* engages in strategic and developmental issues regarding the long-term operation of the whole company or organization. Beside discussing and deciding crucial business matters, it is also involved in building and nurturing a corporate culture — norms, values, and code of conduct — well-adapted to the company goals. Holistic-integrative issues are highly complex, and there are seldom any given solutions to them.

In addition to that, the way single departments and single managers will be affected in the long run is often unpredictable. Thus, and even more than was the case for the problem-solving team, these team members have to put their own interests aside and devote themselves to the success of the company as a whole. They must also feel unimpeded in using their creativity. If they are afraid of losing face or being back-stabbed, they will limit themselves and not bring all their competence and energy to the discussions.

When facing increasing complexity and more demanding customers, many companies have been compelled to give up traditional command-and-control leadership methods in favor of indirect, holistic, and non-directive ones, since the latter are compatible with empowering employees to take more responsibility. Visions, goals, information, feedback, values, and corporate culture have been cited as means for getting people to perform, filling the void after discarding micromanagement. This puts the management in a difficult situation, because everyone knows how command-and-control management is executed. Top management gives clear instructions to the managers at the next level; they pass them on to the people who are supposed to execute the orders from above. The logic is simple and understandable for everyone involved. However, how can a business be controlled by the use of visions or values, and how can a culture that is maximally supporting business success be built and implemented?

Many companies have replaced the obsolete instruments for management and control with more flexible ones, only to find that management has lost its firm grip on the organization. A similar dilemma is familiar to many parents: "I can force him to do his homework, but how can I make him *want* to do it?" There is a risk that they will abdicate their role as fosterers, since the child-rearing practices they were subjected to themselves do not seem to work on the children of today. In my experience, many company managers act in a similar way, using "management-by-e-mail" or other information techniques in a vain hope that people will understand what to do. As we have already established, though: *You cannot lead a complex organization by remote control in a changing world* (Chapter 3 p. 71). Modern leadership calls for closer personal relations, nothing less.

The concept of an empowering leadership style, in contrast to managing by command-and-control, is not new. In 1939, Kurt Lewin divided leadership into three styles: *Autocratic* (in later research, *Authoritarian*), *Democratic*,[63] and *Laissez-faire*. At that time, and especially in the post-war 1950s and 60s, leadership theorists recommended a shift from the prevalent authoritarian style toward a democratic one. The reason, then, was mainly to create a good working environment and improve work satisfaction. Today, when the old "rack-and-pinion-drive"

---

[63] This is not a very well-chosen name, as it is not about everyone having the same influence equally, or about decisions being made by vote. It is, rather, about empowering, *i.e.,* delegating as much decision power as possible to employees—but no more.

logic is too rigid to meet business complexity and customer demands, an empowering leadership style is not just about making employees feel better, it is a powerful tool for keeping up quality and profitability.

In my opinion, as well as from my experience, the solution to this dilemma is to be found in one of the main functions of the *holistic-integrative team*: to promote and implement a strong corporate culture where every action is naturally evaluated against its impact on company success, and where everybody—employees and managers alike—spontaneously takes responsibility for correcting behavior that leads in the opposite direction. Instead of external control through micromanagement, the employees control themselves and each other, based on a profound commitment to company values.

This is easier to say than to do, which is the reason why it is more often said than done. Many companies spend a great deal of time and money on formulating the culture they wish to see, and on spreading these formulations throughout the company. However, very few companies put any effort into the difficult part: to take measures for correcting employees—managers and subordinates— who violate the espoused principles. The reason for this omission is simple. Discussing how things should be is far less sensitive, thus demanding far less openness and trust, than arraigning a misbehaving colleague. As a result, a crucial condition for a successful corporate culture implementation is securing a sufficient level of openness and trust.

To sum up, Diagram 7 shows how the level of openness and trust is linked to Mattsson's three levels of cooperation and four "types" of management teams, and also
to Katzenbach's distinction between single-leader and
real team leadership.

Complexity/ Cooperation	Management Team Type	Leadership	Level of Openness and Trust
Operational tasks/Information exchange	Information team	Single-leader management	Superficial level (Level of Social Convenience)
Complex tactical tasks/ Cooperation	Sounding-board team		Intermediate level
	Problem-solving team		
Strategic and developmental tasks/Close collaboration	Holistic-Integrative team	Real management team	Deep level

Diagram 7. Level of Openness and Trust vs. Team Functioning

The LOT of the management team of Company X

The LOT helix throws a new light on the problems that
became visible in the interviews with the members of
Company X's management team before their offsite

team-building. For example, several members expressed dissatisfaction at the team spending too much time on operational issues, and too little on strategic ones. They had tried to handle this by devoting the last half of the meeting to strategic, *i.e.,* holistic-integrative discussions, but this did not help much. Either these discussions soon turned into debates on some operational aspect of the issue raised, or all of them together just "forgot" that they were to shift focus at half-time. Instead of halting and reflecting on why they did so, they went back to working the way they used to, before. This was done without cancelling the decision to reserve meeting-time for strategic discussions. Thus, they had an agreement that none of them was following, making it justifiable not to bother about other joint agreements.

At this time, we can rephrase the problem of not addressing strategic issues: *the management team was occupying themselves with dealing with operational issues because its level of openness and trust was insufficient for handling more complex ones.* Strategic, holistic-integrative issues imply complexity, unpredictability, and crossing over areas of responsibility; calling for team members to shoulder responsibility beyond the one they have as heads of their departments. Inevitably, this would make them tread on each other's toes, giving rise to infighting and conflicts. The easy way to avoid that from happening is to stick to the well-worn path of operational discussions.

The shallow level of openness and trust is not only a source of problems; it also prevents these problems from being solved. Unable to address the real cause, of not being able to deal with complex issues — the insufficient dynamics of the team — they can do no better than simplify the problem of absent strategy discussions into a matter of scheduling. Here we recognize a familiar characteristic of a team with an insufficient level of openness and trust: trying to solve a dynamic problem by using linear and structural measures (chapter 3, p. 62).

The increasing competence of dealing with complex and sensitive issues as the team goes deeper into the LOT helix is illustrated by the way Jay's concerns about being counteracted are met during the first 24 hours of the team-building. When he raises the issue for the first time, the reactions are defensive; those who felt his criticism was aimed at them countered with excuses and rejection, and the others chose not to insure that the issue was treated seriously, by staying in the bleachers. The next time he was met with more acceptance, mainly because he was more sincere. His daring to show vulnerability is a consequence of a deeper level of openness and trust in the team, but it is also a contribution to bringing the team to an even deeper level. When the team gathers in the morning of the second day, Jay raises the issue a third time, and this time the process level is deep enough for the team to be able to meet him with empathy, and to criticize those who were accused by him of obstructing the decision. However, all the members of the team hesitate to address the more sensitive, underlying issues of power and influence. This leads to the conclusion that they, together, have made substantial progress but still have more work to do, to be able to handle all aspects of their shared reality.

When the team comes together after lunch, the consultants remind them of the overall task for the offsite: to give the necessary feedback to develop efficiency, both within the group and in the company as a whole. Mary, manager of customer relations, picks up the gauntlet by calling attention to an issue that has been bothering her for a while. Half a year ago, the team discussed how to increase sales by encouraging support personnel to ask potential customers, who call seeking support for a product they have purchased, what their needs are for other Company X products. For example, they could interest them in the company's planned product development, and, at the same time, pick up feedback from them to pass on to the production department. The idea was met with unanimous enthusiasm, and they all agreed to implement this new order immediately.

With the exception of some notorious naysayers, the service people in Mary's department received the news of their expanded role positively. However, it soon became clear to them that they had a very diffused notion of the product strategy of the company, i.e., which products were to be improved and which were to be phased out. Mary has continuously tried to keep her direct reports updated on the visions and development plans of the company, but she has gradually become more and more uncertain of what these visions and plans really are. When the visions have been concretized into activities, they have turned out to be contradictory in several cases. Accordingly, she is not sure if she has failed to understand what appears to be crystal clear to the other team members, or if there actually are ambiguities they should straighten out.

One of the consultants asks Mary to express the essence of her feedback, and to whom she wants to address it. She answers that she is talking to all of them, but, if compelled to pick one, she would point to Robert, the production manager: "I've brought this up with you several times, but I can't make out the response I get." When the consultant asks, "What response do you get?" Mary tries to describe the "we do as we always have done" attitude that she is met with whenever she approaches Robert and others in his department.

Robert answers that the company's product strategy is crystal clear to him and to everyone at the production department. He can't understand what Mary's problem is. When she persists, asking him what consequences the long-term visions of the company have on everyday production, Robert brushes her aside, claiming that the visions are nothing but idle wishes for the future, calling for no immediate action. John supports Mary's opinion that there is uncertainty about where the company is going in the future, but he and his marketing guys handle that by focusing on what is already "on the shelves." However, he foresees a risk of Company X losing market shares to its competitors in the long run, since the latter seem to be more agile when it comes to launching new products.

The other team members join the discussion, suggesting different interpretations of the purport of the company's visions and strategies. Richard is acting defensively, since he perceives the discussion as questioning his leadership. He explains his views of the future for the company, and its implications for each department. "We have unanimously agreed on this," he declares, looking around the team. "I can't understand why this is coming up again." Mary ignores the implicit message—that she should be ashamed of bringing the subject up— and she persists in claiming that the discussion has not made her any wiser.

The consultants point to the fact that team members take the liberty of interpreting the company strategy their own way, without exploring their differences and the personal needs and hidden agendas behind these differences. Their intervention opens up for reflection and tentative efforts to look into their different views. Richard persists in asserting that they are wasting time on a pseudo-problem, since they all agreed when the strategy was discussed and decided. However, he has no good answer to what the real problem is, since the issue is being actualized again. John states an opinion that the others have heard before: that the business strategy includes too many services and products, making it incoherent and diffuse. He argues for focusing on some of them and outsourcing the rest to sub-contractors. This leads to a heated discussion. Mary and Susan go along with John, while Robert, Richard, and Jay are more skeptical. Victor says something about traditions and "the spirit of the company," but no one understands what he is trying to convey, or which side in the discussion he is taking. He gets a caustic remark from John and decides not to take part in any further discussion. Jane expresses no opinion of her own; instead, as usual, she tries to mediate between the two sides. Eventually, the discussion is interrupted by dinner break.

After dinner, the discussion gradually turns into a general debate on strategy practicalities. The emerging attention to how they influence each other in the team seems to have vanished. To bring them back on that track, the consultants persistently invite them to give each other direct feedback on their behavior here and now. This unleashes attacking and counter-attacking, mainly between John and Mary on one side, and Robert and Jay on the other. The rest of the team assume spectator roles.

Jay turns to Mary, accusing her of having been generally negative and rather condescending to him at a meeting half a year ago. Mary takes a defensive position, and their dispute gets caught in a fruitless discussion about what was said at that time and what was not. The consultants' attempts to shift attention toward what is happening in the room at this moment has little impact. The person they turn to answers dutifully, only to plunge into the dispute again. Obviously, the inclination for reflection and self-criticism is low at the moment.

Eventually, they have emptied their verbal magazines and are repeating themselves. Those not directly involved in the bickering lose interest, since it doesn't seem to lead anywhere. Someone invites the team to discuss a less combustible topic, but the response is wan; the feeling of discouragement falling on the team chokes every attempt to take the discussion anywhere else. Jane's suggestion that they should use the time for planning their upcoming customer event is totally ignored. The consultants state matter-of-factly that the team is stuck. When that commentary is followed by more or less subtle pleas for help, the consultants choose to leave the room.

Undoubtedly, those active in the discussion are giving each other frank and unsparing feedback. In comparison with the previous reluctance to address each other directly, this must be seen as an improvement. However, there is a snag in it: it is as if everyone is talking and no one is listening. Indeed, every person hears the words coming from the others, but only in relation to their own arguments. In that way, they reduce their teammates to antagonists in their own inner conflict scenarios. This way of relating to others is a kind of *self-reference*: I attribute a role based on my perception of reality to someone, and I interact with that role, oblivious of the fact that it consists of my own projections onto the other person. Actually, I am talking to myself—or more precisely, to a creation of my imagination—rather than to the other person in his own right.

The self-referential quality of the feedback renders it toothless in spite of the bold criticism. At this point, the team has found a way to treat feedback as a game, a spectacle not to be taken too seriously. The similarity to how jargon is used in workplaces is striking (chapter 5, p. 155). There is a subtext saying that it is only a show and no one is supposed to take it personally.

A crucial step in the development process of the management team is learning the difference between the fierce wrangling they are into now, and genuine feedback. The distinctive feature of genuine feedback is that *the sender makes himself vulnerable*. Rapping out "truths" and "frank comments," protecting oneself in a trench of self-righteousness, is of no value whatsoever to the people around, and, of course, it has no value to the sender of this kind of "feedback," either.

Learning to use genuine feedback is not an intellectual process; if it were that simple, the consultants could have used their authority to interfere with the discussion and start lecturing on the principles of good communication well before now. The understanding gained that way might be used in a civilized discussion, but it would have vanished into thin air the next time the team plunged into an emotional turmoil like the one they are in at the moment. Really to learn from this experience, they have to go deeper into it, not be saved from it. In this perspective, the increasing frustration is a godsend, since frustration is a very potent fuel for change. The intention behind the consultants' leaving the room is to reinforce that frustration, and, at the same time, to emphasize that the team has to take full responsibility for dealing with it.

When the consultants return to the team some 20 minutes later, the frustration over not having gotten any further has increased. Richard has resumed his formal role as manager, trying to arouse enthusiasm for some financial issues, but not even Victor seems interested, in spite of the fact that he, in his role as financial manager, has raised the same issues at previous meetings. His facial expressions alternate between resignation and irritation, but he does nothing to lead the conversation in some other direction. John looks more and more desperate, and, eventually, begins to answer Richard back, just to spark the discussion. Jay steps in with a report on the development of costs in the IT department, but no one seems to catch what he is trying to say. Mark describes a course in coaching that he has attended, but he stops when no one takes notice of him. Jane looks miserable, and Susan is self-absorbed. Robert and Mary try to keep their conflict going, but their agitated voices cannot conceal that their dispute is going in circles.

Unlike previous deadlocks, at this time there is a great deal of emotional energy, but the team cannot canalize it constructively. It is like an engine that is being revved up, but no one knows how to put the car in first gear.

Victor has been silent for a long time, but his face reveals that he is very uncomfortable. Jane notices that, and asks how he is. He answers, "I don't understand; I mean, what are we doing?" He looks around before going on: "No one seems to give a shit about anyone here, except for himself." Now he has caught the attention of everyone in the room, not so much because of what he is saying, but because of his having emphasized every word. Obviously, he has a lot on his mind, and he is letting it all out. After describing how depressing the actual situation in the team is to him, he continues with telling them about how badly he was treated by Richard's predecessor as CEO, and how he has kept a low profile since then. He is heartily sick of the obscure role he has taken in the management team up until now. He gives several examples of how he has been steamrolled when he has not been assertive enough, not only by Richard but by several other team members as well. Deep down he is really angry with the others, but most of all he is disappointed with himself for allowing it to happen.

The force of Victor's outburst takes everyone aback. Eventually, Robert gives Victor credit for being so frank, and adds that he has sensed aggressiveness behind Victor's gentle facade. Nods from the others confirm that Robert is not the only one who has felt that way. Several others begin, tentatively, to scrutinize the ways they have been acting toward Victor. Susan says that she can recognize herself in Victor's statement; she is also trying to be tough by not showing when she feels hurt. After making sure that her shifting the focus to herself is okay with Victor, she says that she has been under great pressure for a long time, at work as well as at home. Tears show in her eyes, and, as Jay is stating the obvious — that she looks sad — she answers that most of all she feels relieved. She repeats what she said the day before, that she feels that John and Robert have treated her badly, and this time both of them listen seriously to her without getting defensive. The other team members support her and Victor by listening empathetically, and by sharing reflections of their own.

John admits that he has not been fair to Susan but alleges, by way of an excuse, that he has had a rough time, too. After a moment of hesitation and inner struggle, he reveals that he has already spoiled one marriage by working too much and spending too little time with his family. Now, the same thing is happening again. A daughter from his first marriage contracted an eating disorder, and his ex-wife has insinuated that it is because John has not involved himself enough with her. He has tried to spend as much time as possible with her, only to face accusations from his second wife, that he is neglecting his present family. Because of this, his second wife has moved into her mother's house, taking their children with her.

John's candor paves the way for the team members to tell each other about their life situations, and the price they all pay for allowing work to be such a big part of their lives. Most of them are struggling with family problems, and, as was the case with John, they have concealed their problems from the other team members. An insight is surfacing in the team, and it is put into words by Robert: "It is not just the workload in itself that weighs heavy on us. It is having to keep up appearances, as if we are not having any trouble at all, and pretending to be invincible."

The consultants have remained passive ever since Victor had his outburst, and, obviously, the team needs no interference from them at this moment. Eventually, they choose to leave the room, indicating that they have full confidence in the team members' competence to handle the process by themselves. They stay outside the room until the team chooses to break up; the clock shows half past one in the morning.

Now, we can follow the management team as it takes further steps toward improving their cooperative process. The level of openness and trust characterizing the team just after dinner was indeed sufficient to allow important issues to come up, but not yet adequate for making it possible to talk about those issues in a meaningful way. This has fomented a growing frustration, which turned out to be a strong driving force to get further into the process. When the frustration gets strong enough, it propels a breakthrough, in contrast to the previous step-by-step development. The team members feel as if a door is opened to a world that has previously been inaccessible to them.

Victor is the one breaking the ice, letting his frustration out, but it could just as well have been Susan or John bursting first. What is important is the outcome: the team members begin to let go of the masks they have been hiding their true feelings behind. This is a huge step from where they were at the outset of the development process. However, the final test is still to come—making use of their newborn openness when addressing the problems that curb the prosperity of Company X.

CHAPTER 7.
THE OUTCOME OF THE TEAM DEVELOPMENT PROCESS

When the team comes together on the morning of the third day, the atmosphere is marked by the strong feelings of the evening before. They seem to be tired and a bit confused, but at the same time, the air is filled with new feelings of expectation and optimism. Their hesitation, when the consultants ask them to reflect on the team development process as they did the morning before, is caused by an almost solemn atmosphere. Gone is the earlier reluctance to share their experiences.

Mary begins, telling how relieved she feels to be able to speak her mind, not having to watch her tongue anymore. She has often been critical of the way the team has worked, but most of the time she has kept that to herself, or expressed it only hintingly. Now, she realizes that, by doing so, she has contributed to the negative team atmosphere.

She also understands that she has not been the only one questioning how the management team have acted as leaders of the company, and that, had she expressed her criticism more clearly, it might have been endorsed by those other members.

Victor and Susan say they recognize themselves in Mary's statement, both in having been reluctant about pointing to the flaws of the team and in being relieved by the group climate, which is now much more open. Victor likens the feeling to having been able to lift a heavy knapsack off his shoulders. He reports he was awake most of the night, seeing different episodes of his years with Company X in his mind's eye—injuries and injustices flashed by—and, suddenly, he realized that they belong to the past and have no importance to him any longer.

Several of the others share Victor's feelings with their own smiles of recognition. Robert makes a wan attempt to laugh the discussion off, but everyone can see that he is deeply moved by what is happening. They all know Robert avoids talking about feelings, in spite of his being the most temperamental among them. However, instead of just noticing that for a fact, as they might have before, the others now help Robert put into words his thoughts about his role in the team, and in the company generally. He becomes serious, admitting that he has thought a lot about how they treat each other at the production department. "I've always thought we are honest and outspoken with each other, but now I'm beginning to wonder if that has just been a pretense, if we've been hiding behind facetious jargon." He quickly adds that the spirit among his co-workers is positive in many ways, and that it won't be easily changed, and he ponders that, perhaps, that kind of change would cause more harm than good. Susan responds by relating how she and her co-workers react when they encounter that kind of jargon in the production department. In the past, they have perceived it as an invincible wall, effectually preventing her and her human resource specialists from doing their jobs.

John reports that he has been thinking about what is important in life, in general, and how he can create a better balance between his work and family. He woke up early and had a long telephone call with his wife. Now, he admits, he is torn between a wish to go home, to go on talking with her, and a strong desire to continue the team process. He is also beginning to see his restlessness in a new light. Before, everything seemed simple: he was the promoter and the others were sluggish or reluctant. These days, he has, for the first time, experienced that his restlessness is actually an impediment for him getting what he wants, both because he has been building resistance in the people around him, and because it has been blocking his ability to see alternative ways to proceed. The insight that the problem might be his own behavior came to him when he got almost exactly the same feedback from his wife as he had gotten the day before from the other members of the management team.

Jay says that listening to the others, and to John in particular, has stirred up many thoughts in him. He is the youngest member of the team, both in age and in years as a leader, so he has not seen the drawbacks of having leadership responsibility as clearly as the others. He starts talking about his family situation, but only half-heartedly. Jane frowns, saying that it seems as if Jay thinks he is expected to share details from his personal life just because others have done that. In response, Jay breaks off, looking, suddenly, confused. One of the consultants intervenes, saying that telling about one's private life is not necessarily the same as personal openness, which makes Jay realize that he was trying to take a shortcut into the team's spirit of community, and that it will take much more than that if he is to hang onto the rapid development of the team at this moment.

Jane follows him, describing how the anxiety she has felt for a long time—and, increasingly, during the first two days of their offsite—has now ceased. She is filled with a feeling of peace and determination, although she cannot put her finger on any particular reason for it. Her only concern is about Richard. He has stayed in the background since yesterday, and she wonders why and what consequences this will have in the future, on his role as leader of the management team.

Richard nods at Jane, but instead of answering her questions, he says that what he sees in the team at the moment is exactly what he wished for: they are paying attention to each other, sharing commitment, straightforwardness, and a strong feeling of togetherness. As for himself, he is struggling with how his role as CEO can be adjusted to the newly acquired openness of the team. He is beginning to realize that the distance he has been keeping, in order not to lose respect from the others, has had rather the opposite effect. In the last days, he has experienced being respected most when he was letting go of control and showing his real self. What he previously saw as "losing face" was, in reality, losing the mask that was hiding his true face. However, he realizes that he, in spite of this insight, has a tendency to fall back into his old behavior, and he hopes that the others will let him know when that happens.

Richard's reflections inspire the others to discuss how they relate to their direct reports and the benefits and risks of having a more personal relationship with them. Susan admits that she is sometimes compelled to act more formally toward her subordinates than she wants to, to avoid being accused of favoritism. Jane reports a similar predicament, and adds that preferential treatment is especially sensitive in a workplace with many women, as is the case in the administrative and personnel departments. This sparks quite a stereotyped gender discussion, which Mary interrupts by asking Susan if her need for distance has more to do with herself than with the fact that there are many women in her department.

Mary says she has sensed that Susan has a strong wish to be infallible, which causes her to withdraw to avoid showing vulnerability when she cannot cope with a situation. Susan acknowledges Mary's description of her and turns back to reflecting over her own behavior. Mary becomes so eager in her wish to help Susan sort this out that it soon becomes evident that Mary has an agenda of her own. After Mary's tough feedback, one of the consultants asks Mary, "Are you talking about yourself?" Only then does Mary realize that much of her "feedback" to Susan is actually projections of traits of her own, and she starts talking about herself instead. She reveals that she sometimes panics when people come too close to her, because she is uncertain of what she is committing herself to by allowing them to do so. Mary's contribution introduces fear as a topic, and several of the others catch on, sharing their experiences of situations when they, too, have been scared.

Mark, the purchasing manager, has been quiet since the reflection session started. Eventually, Susan turns to him to ask, "What are you afraid of?" He quickly answers that he is not particularly afraid. He feels safe with his job and with the people around him. At the same time, her question has brought an anxious expression to his face. He quickly composes his features, regaining the indifferent expression they all are familiar with, but no one could miss catching the glimpse of uneasiness in his face. No one comments about it, but the team falls silent. Eventually, one of the consultants asks them, "Do you believe him?" They hesitate until, eventually, Robert says, "I don't think that you are as indifferent as you are trying to look." The others nod affirmatively, and Jane says, "It feels rather odd that you are so silent when the team is gathered, because during the breaks you have a lot to say about what is going on. Why don't you bring that up here, instead?" Mark has no answer, but he looks more and more uncomfortable. Mary states that she is often unsure of what is really on his mind, and that she finds it difficult to trust him. She brings up a previous episode, when Mark had promised to back her up but had backed off when he was met with opposition from Richard. "And what about here and now?" one of the consultants asks. "Do you trust him right now?" Mary answers that Mark is the team member she has the least trust in at the moment.

Susan turns to Mark: "Actually, I'm quite mad at you. We are trying to be as open as we can, but you are hiding behind an attitude." Mark, looking more and more uneasy, gets himself entangled in a long, defensive speech, saying that he has always been loyal to the company, and that he has been obliged to solve problems in his own way because the others have failed to back him up. Gradually, his defense morphs into a counterattack on Mary, with Jay and Susan getting their share as well, until Mark finally concludes that, perhaps, he is not pleasing the others, but what is most important to him is that his job gets done.

One of the consultants says calmly: "From what I've heard, I'm not sure that you're doing your job so well." He refers to what transpired from the interviews with the other team members, as well as to financial reports that showed the purchasing department is far from reaching its goals. "Moreover," he continues, "the feedback you are getting here indicates that you are more focused on sucking up to your colleagues than on performing."

The consultant's bringing the feedback to Mark to a head unleashes a torrent of feedback from his fellow team members. Some of it is about his inadequate performance as purchasing manager, and some concerns his manipulative way of trying to tie them up with secrets said "in confidence." In an attempt to escape the spotlight, Mark hints at critical remarks other team members have made about each other, but they regard his doing that as just another example of the kind of manipulations they are trying to force him to acknowledge. The consultants do what they can to help him, telling him just to listen to the feedback he is being given without defending himself, but that does not work. Mark keeps on justifying his behavior, attaining nothing but a growing skepticism from the others.

Richard says he is pleased that the issue of how Mark is leading the purchasing department is on the table, and he claims that he has discussed this with Mark several times. When Mary asks why the problems of the purchasing department remain unresolved if Richard has addressed them as clearly as he now asserts he has, it becomes Richard's turn to become defensive.

Eventually, he calms down and listens to Mary's and the others' thoughts about how his behavior sometimes blurs his messages. They say that, mainly, it is because of his "forgetting" to follow up that his intentions fail to be carried through to completion. Moreover, his not showing a distinct reaction when someone acts counter to instructions he has given them is perceived as a contradictory message by his reports. When he offers, by way of explanation, that, "You have to trust people to do what they have agreed to do," the team does not buy it. Instead, they maintain that the lack of follow-up is a weak spot in Richard's leadership that he should do something about.

Mark has had a respite while Richard has been in the spotlight. Now, Jane asks how he feels, and he responds by resuming his defensive argumentation. One of the consultants interferes, saying that the question was what he feels, not what he thinks. After avoiding answering the question several times, Mark finally says, "Of course, it feels like shit," only to go back to justifying his behavior. It is clear to the consultants that the others are beginning to give up trying to get through to him, and a spirit of discouragement falls on the team.

Until now, the frustration of the team members has been propelling the team development process. At this moment, however, it runs the risk of causing a deadlock, since the team members are about to give up on Mark. To keep up the steam, the consultants invite the members to rank each other on a scale of who they trust most to the one they trust the least. Each members' ranking of the others is written on a flip-chart, and the ranking points for each member is summed up, showing his or her relative status in the team. The result shows that Victor is the most trusted of them, closely followed by Richard. Jay is ranked next to last, and Mark holds the bottom place by a wide margin.

After showing the result, one of the consultants asks where they want to draw the line between an acceptable and unacceptable amount of trust; they agree that the line should be drawn between Jay and Mark. The other consultant pulls Mark's chair out about a yard, placing him outside the group, saying: "This is how I perceive your team at this moment."

They all look taken by surprise, and fall silent. Eventually, Robert breaks the silence: "What shall we do about this situation?" The consultant answers that it is up to Mark to regain his position as one of the team. "But how?" Jane asks. "By doing whatever it takes for you to trust him," is the answer. Mark asks what he should do, but the only answer he gets from the consultant is: "It's your responsibility to find that out."

Jay is preoccupied by the fact that he is the least trusted, second to Mark, and wants to know why. The feedback from the others is about a streak of boyishness that sometimes comes out as inattention and irresponsibility, and that he also has a tendency to keep several options open by not revealing his opinion when they are discussing an issue. These things together make the other team members unsure of when to trust him, and not. Jay listens thoughtfully and says that he recognizes himself in their criticism of him, and that he wants to change for the better. Victor tells Jay that his trust in him has already increased because of the way he asks for and receives feedback. The others agree.

The discussion during the rest of the day is mainly about how to handle the situation at Company X when they return to work. Now and then, they come back to Mark, who is still sitting outside the group, but no one sees any solution to the locked situation. Mark gives some faint promises to change his behavior, but it is only Jane who shows any inclination to take that as a pretext to invite him back to the team. The others persist in wanting to see his new behavior in action before they will believe him.

When the offsite session is drawing to an end, Richard asks for a talk in private with the consultants. He wants advice about how to handle the situation with Mark being placed outside the team, and he suggests that it might be a good idea to invite him back in before they leave. The consultants answer that they think that would be a bad idea, for at least two reasons. First, it would be lowering the bar for what it takes to be qualified as a member of the management team, which would be tantamount to returning the team back to their previous inefficient way of functioning; and, second, returning Mark now would be depriving him of an opportunity to grow as a person and a leader. Instead, they instruct Richard to monitor the aftermath very closely. Obviously, Mark will need intense coaching, which would give him an opportunity to sort out the feedback he has received, but it is also important to remain vigilant about the tendencies for scapegoating and rejection on the parts of the other team members. "The present situation with Mark outside the team is no fake or consultant gimmick," they conclude. "It is a reflection of reality, and it has to be resolved properly."

That the team members are able to speak openly about their fears in different situations is a confirmation of the deep level of openness and trust that they have already attained. They are in a positive helix, where openness reinforces trust and trust reinforces openness. Indeed, the superficial gender discussion that arose between Jane and Susan might be seen as a way to escape deeper issues. However, it was soon expanded by Mary to include the subject of fear, which enabled several others to share their own experiences with the team.

The task of the consultants at this stage is mostly to endorse what the team members are doing by pointing to behaviors that support the positive group climate. Their aim is to increase the members' awareness of what behavior deepens the process, and what behavior takes them in the opposite direction. This is in line with the main goal of the offsite, that the team members gain competence to secure a sufficient level of openness and trust by themselves. At this moment, that competence still needs support from the outside, since it has been recently gained

and, therefore, is still poorly anchored in their cooperative culture. Their need for support is exemplified by the
fact that no one spontaneously points to the obvious mis-
match between Mark's anxious body language and his
verbal declaration that everything is okay. However, with
a little help from the consultants, they are able to address
this incongruence, as well as the anxiety behind it. For
the moment, the team members can depend on receiving
similar pushes whenever they backslide to a too superficial process level. The long-term goal, however, is that
the external help will become unnecessary.

Another confirmation of the deeper process level of
the team is that they are able to address an issue they
have been avoiding until then, namely, Mark's inadequate
performance and his manipulative way of keeping that
issue out of the discussion. As a consequence of increased
openness and trust, and the heightened attention to each
other that is the hallmark of that, the detrimental effects
of Mark's behavior have become evident to his fellow
management team members. The fact that one of the consultants brings the issue to a head does not matter much;
it is more important that it is brought up. The consultant's intervention was based on his assumption that the
level of openness and trust was sufficient for the team
to be able to handle that sensitive issue constructively.
By intervening, he paves the way for the team members
to address issues they have previously been "forbidden"
to discuss.

Group pressure: legitimate claiming or bullying?

There are many aspects of both the team's and the consultants' behavior toward Mark that calls for clarification. The group pressure directed at him is strong and, obviously, he is feeling attacked and exposed by everyone else in the room. The consultants' interventions do nothing to reduce the pressure on him — quite the contrary. At a cursory glance, this could easily be mistaken for bullying, a phenomenon not unusual in workplace teams. Therefore, it is highly important to understand how confronting feedback differs from a rejection process.

The conclusive difference has to do with the purpose of exposing a person to group pressure. The members of the management team of Company X give Mark merciless feedback to afford him an opportunity to learn and to change, hoping that it will help him fulfill his role as a management team member and head of the purchasing department. The fact that they do not back off — in spite of Mark's defending himself frenetically — is actually proof of their consideration for him. It would be much easier just to conclude that they do not trust him and leave it to Richard to remove him from his position. At a superficial glance, this might be regarded as more merciful, since it will spare Mark the unpleasantness of being targeted by his team colleagues. However, in reality, this would be far more ruthless, since it would deprive him of both a chance to regain the trust he has lost and an opportunity to learn from the situation. Sparing him that experience would be a perfect example of the "ruthless consideration" referred to in chapter 5 (p. 160).

Bullying and scapegoating in a workplace team is something totally different from constructive feedback. The purpose of the former is to identify a scapegoat onto whom the others can project their shortcomings, thus getting rid of their own feelings of powerlessness, incompetence, dissatisfaction, and guilt. The aim is to use the scapegoat as a trash can for everything that is not okay; it is not intended to give him an opportunity to learn and grow. The acting is, in fact, for the benefit of the actor and not of the person being acted against. The targeted person is excluded from the group, either mentally, by being shut out from genuine contact with the other members, or physically, by actually being removed from their presence. The primitive fantasy propelling an exclusion process is that the expelled person will take away the "bad" when he leaves, placing it outside the group, while the "good" remains on the inside. However, the relief from getting rid of what is allegedly causing the group trouble in this way is of very short duration and, once this pattern of problem "solving" is established, the search for a new scapegoat soon begins again. As a natural consequence, no one takes the risk of showing his or her true self in such a group climate, which severely restricts any opportunity for one to learn from the consequences of his actions.

Theoretically, there is a vast difference between giving pure feedback and projecting one's own undesired features onto someone else.[64] In real life, however, the difference might be quite subtle. An important task for the consultants during a team process like this is to be vigilant about projective aspects polluting given feedback. For example, if one of Mark's fellow team members gets a little too keen on giving him feedback, or makes distant or crushing remarks, there is a good reason to suspect that he is using Mark as a means to reduce his own feelings of frustration, or to deflect attention from her own shortcomings. Mary's feedback to Susan about her need for distance from her co-workers, above, might be seen as a mild form of projection, since she takes advantage of Susan's initiative to talk indirectly about herself without making herself vulnerable.

The consultants' persistently pointing at everything they consider as projections is not only a way to prevent the team process from getting obscured, it is also designed to grow the members' ability to recognize projections and other defense mechanisms whenever they may be resorting to these. In the end, the consultants hope to make themselves redundant in this respect, transferring the responsibility for monitoring and improving communication and cooperation skills to the team members. This self-correcting ability is a crucial aspect of the competence the team needs to attain in order to be able to secure

---

[64] See Appendix, p. 292, for a definition of *projection*.

a level of openness and trust sufficient for performing adequately when they return to their workaday lives.

The ranking of the team members' trust in each other is a potent way of bringing the process further when, otherwise, there is a risk that it will come to a halt. The purpose is to make the situation so obvious that no one can escape dealing with it, thus preventing the team from sliding back to their previous approach, i.e., to ignore what all of them see as a problem if it is too sensitive to address. The consultants supply the method, but they do not evaluate single team members or try to influence the setting of a standard for what behavior is acceptable, or not. They stand firmly behind one clear principle: insights must lead to consistent action. Pulling Mark's chair out of the circle is making that principle come to life. Again, it is about visualizing the existing reality, not trying to push that reality in a specific direction. Perhaps someone might think that moving his chair is unnecessarily remorseless, but the consultants considered the alternative crueler. It would cause Mark to become isolated in the team with no chance to regain the trust of the others.

Should feedback be given within the team, or one-on-one?

Many leaders, and consultants, assert that feedback should be given one-on-one and not in a team context, especially when the feedback might be sensitive or regarded as criticism. The argument for this position is that the receiver will feel less exposed, making him less defensive and more disposed for a constructive dialog. Indeed, face-to-face feedback is less challenging for both sender and receiver. Furthermore, the level of openness and trust in most workplace teams is too shallow to make team feedback ethically and effectually recommendable. Members of teams with insufficient levels of openness and trust will lack awareness of projections and infighting, making them unable to separate constructive feedback from bullying and scapegoating.

However, on the condition that the Company X team has reached a sufficient level of openness and trust, there are several benefits from being able to criticize and to endorse each other within the context of the full team. The most important are:

Feedback becomes more exhaustive and differentiated. Feedback from several people brings out a diversity of aspects and perspectives, causing the message to become more nuanced. As mentioned earlier (p. 15), feedback is essentially information about the impact a person's behavior has on other people and on the working process. The variety of responses is also important to enabling a person to understand his role and influence. It is most unlikely that all team members will perceive the behavior of one of its members in exactly the same way; if they should do so, it would likely be a sign of the kind of bullying and scapegoating described above.

Less risk of infighting or hidden alliances, which distort the message. The interaction between two people is commonly influenced by competition, tactical considerations, or shared beliefs that neither is aware of. Within a group, especially one that shares a deep level of openness and trust, there is a fair chance that someone from the outside can interject a perspective of the communication between two members that will debunk manipulations and hidden agendas. Otherwise, there is a risk that seemingly honest feedback may become a subtle means to exert power, or a manifestation of an agreement—deliberate or subconscious—to spare each other unpleasant truths. In a well-functioning team, members themselves help each other to keep their feedback clean from these kinds of distortions.

Feedback in a team context promotes learning for all members. Open exchange of feedback makes it possible for all team members to better understand the reality in which they are participating. Truly, no man is an island; it is not possible to understand human behavior independent of context. In the example above, Richard is sure that he has been acting firmly on Mark's inadequate performance, yet he has no convincing answer when asked what action he took when he, in spite of his claim, saw no progress in Mark's behavior. At that point, it became clear to all of them that Richard's behavior was contributing to Mark's problems not being solved, and he has to reconsider his way of handling the situation. Similarly, the other team members can be held accountable for letting the unsatisfactory state of things go on, despite their knowledge of them. This does not reduce Mark's obligation; responsibility in a team context is no zero-sum game in which an increase in one person's responsibility reduces someone else's. On the contrary, he or she who omits doing everything possible to put an end to misconduct is sharing the responsibility, even if someone else is formally accountable.

Richard's alleging that he has confronted Mark is an example of how our apprehension of our own behavior is easily infiltrated by wishful thinking, especially when we feel obliged to handle unpleasant issues. After balking about having to raise the issue with Mark for weeks, Richard realized he could not avoid it any longer. When he brought it up at last, he had built up so much anxiety that he simply accepted Mark's promises of improvement, with great relief. While the feeling of relief is understandable, it is not acceptable that he blinked at no real change of behavior following Mark's promises. Moreover, when criticized by the other team members for not following up Mark's response to his demands, Richard alleged that his not doing so was because he has confidence in his direct reports. Indeed, having that is a good thing in itself, but in this case he actually used a defensive maneuver we previously identified, in chapter 5: describing shortcomings and incapacities as if they were virtues. However, Richard's chance to get away with that without becoming a target of frank feedback is minimal in the light of the profound level of openness and trust that characterizes his management team at this point.

Probability increases that feedback will lead to action. It is well-known that promises made in a team context are more obliging than those made face-to-face. The person who does not fulfill his obligations will have several people keeping an eye on him, and he also runs the risk of being subjected to group pressure, which can be very unpleasant. Facing the risk of being held accountable for one's actions — or lack of actions — by a group of persistent people, most people will make an extra effort to fulfill their commitments.

Open feedback creates and maintains a positive corporate culture. As I mentioned before (p. 212), one of the most important strategic tasks of a management team is creating and maintaining a corporate culture that supports business success. Top management in many companies advocate frank and honest communication, but too often they foil their own good intentions by failing to "walk the talk." It is inevitable that the employees will adopt the level of openness shown by management in action, not that preached to them in formal declarations. Therefore, it is crucial for members of a management team to secure a sufficient level of openness and trust in their own team before even trying to make it a policy for the whole company. Actions speak louder than words; top managers not only talking about openness but also practicing it in the management team will bring that openness to their departments by example, instead of by persuasion. This is a far more efficient way of implementing culture than trumpeting governing principles.

When striving toward an open team climate, one has to be aware of the risk of creating a culture of "pseudo-openness," which is just as stereotyped as the distrustful culture they wish to abandon. In chapter 6 (p. 233), Jay noticed that John got positive reactions on being open about his family situation and saw that as evidence that those kinds of revelations were an admission ticket to the spirit of community in the team. He did not notice, however, that John's openness regarded something very emotional to him, while his own "openness" was merely an attempt to suck up to the others. His immaturity, lack of life experience, or his having lived in an environment sparing him from feedback causes him not to realize that the people around him intuitively sense the difference between genuine and tactical openness.

It is not unusual for members of a team undergoing team development to interpret the situation the same way Jay does in the example above. There is a small step from that to considering what was forbidden before as mandatory now for anyone wanting to be part of the team. What started as an act of liberation, then, can easily be turned into another constraint: the personal openness they wanted is replaced by a ritualistic "openness" behind which they, once again, can hide. A mask of tears, or of spicy revelations, can be as effective as a stone face when it comes to hiding one's true self.

The breaking-up of the offsite

When the team broke up after three days of team-building, the situation was far from stable. Someone might find it disturbing that the consultants did nothing to secure the team members leaving the event with a good feeling by resolving the situation of Mark's exclusion from the team. However, their choice of action was a consequence of their assignment, and of the philosophy on which they found their approach. It would certainly have been an immediate relief to the team members if the consultants had come up with some kind of "soft landing," putting the conflicts aside, at least symbolically. However, such an intervention would not have helped the team in the long run. Rather, the tension and frustration in the team is a strong driving force toward the change that will be necessary to make Company X as successful as they all want it to be. Discharging that force by trivializing, softening, or nullifying the frank feedback given, especially to Mark, would not only reduce the benefit from the three days offsite, it would fuel the feeling that it is pointless to raise controversial issues, since they come to nothing anyway. In the long run, this would be a far worse outcome. Faithful to the purpose of their assignment, then, the consultants would do everything they can to support the situation being resolved by real change, rather than by smoothing things over or putting a lid on what is unpleasant.

Moreover, these three days are just the beginning of a development program that will extend over at least a year. From that perspective, the situation is only temporarily unresolved.

The aim of these three initial days of working with the team process has been to break up ingrained attitudes, and to give the team members an opportunity to experience more constructive ways of dealing with complex and sensitive issues. Operative matters have not been focused on. On the contrary, the consultants have done all they can to keep them out of the discussion. The reason for that is, metaphorically, the same reason why you put the gear into neutral when you tune-up the engine of a car. The purpose is not to get from one place to another, but to have a tiptop engine when it is time to leave. No driver would drive with only three valves working, arguing that it takes too much time to get the car fixed—at least not if he is about to make a long trip. However, such arguments are not unusual in management teams: "We have no time for shaping our management team; we are too busy keeping up with what's happening in the market."

That said, the situation would have been quite different if the aim of the offsite had been for the team members to learn communication techniques. In that case, it would have been reasonable to discharge the tension between Mark and the rest of the team, for example, by admitting him to the team with some wishful comments that he would probably just have to digest what the others had told him. In that situation, the educational goal would be reached when the team members expressed their feedback to Mark, and he acknowledged hearing it.

However, in a development process like this, communication is a means, not a goal in itself. Company X needs more than good communication between its managers to be competitive. The words must lead to action that will propel the enterprise in the right direction. There is still work to do before the engine will purr like a kitten, to complete the metaphor above, but, nonetheless, it is time to put the car in first gear by transforming their gained insights into productive activity. There are still many unresolved conflicts and other impediments to company success that have to be dealt with, and many strategic issues are yet to be solved. In addition to that, the overall building of a strong and purposive corporate culture remains. The real challenges are still to come, in spite of the intense work the team members have done together over these three days.

What happened next

Before leaving the offsite venue, management team members agree to meet for a follow-up as soon as possible, both because of the instability of the team, and also because of their genuine wish to enjoy the deep feeling of togetherness they have created. Wednesday, the week after the offsite, they all meet in their regular conference room at Company X, except for Susan, who had planned a week off long before. One of the consultants participates, too.

Richard begins by reporting that he had felt shaken and confused when he left the offsite. When he arrived home, his wife of 27 years immediately saw that something had happened, so he tried to explain what he had been through. It had not been easy. Indeed, he could describe things that had been said and done, but that did not seem fully to explain the emotional turmoil he was going through. His wife had listened patiently and finally said she did not quite grasp what he was saying, although she could see that something important had happened. After that, Richard says, they talked for many hours about dreams, expectations, and disappointments in their lives, and other things they had not discussed in years, and he reveals that they have not been so close in years. Afterward, they made love for the first time in several months, which Richard chooses to keep to himself. To conclude, he says that he is very hopeful of Company X's future, and he is convinced that their operation will gain speed, as he has wished. Someone asks him what makes him hopeful, and he answers that they really have gotten to know each other through the days at the offsite, and this has made it possible for them to get straight to the point when it comes to making things happen at the company.

Mary is next. She tells that she went to see John the first thing Monday morning, to discuss how they could improve the coordination of their departments. "We looked at each other," she says, smiling, "and I think both of us felt ashamed of not having been able to solve this before. At least I felt that way." They describe broadly what they have agreed upon, and several of the others endorse it by saying that it sounds as if they really are going to carry it out. Their credibility in the eyes of the others is increased considerably, more from their determination and profound mutual understanding than from the words of promise they use.

John reports he spent the weekend talking with his wife about their marriage, and they both agreed they did not want to spoil the years they have had together. He also spent more time with his children than he usually does on the weekends. He had a sincere talk with his 13-year old son, which he has not done in a very long time, and which made him realize how little he knew about what went on in the boy's head.

Many of the other team members report similar experiences of coming closer to their family members. Victor describes it as "opening a door that has been closed for a long time." He spent the weekend with his children from his former marriage, and he describes how he was much more relaxed and present than he used to be when he meets them every fortnight, and that they had responded by being less demanding and jealous of each other. When he came to work Monday morning, he felt an urge to tell his co-workers what he has been going through, so he decided to use his Monday morning meeting with his direct reports to do that, putting the usual financial issues aside. "I couldn't explain to them what happened between us in the management team," he continues, "so I decided to try and describe what I learned about myself and in what respect I want to become a better leader. I was afraid they would think I was being too personal, because I told them I had lost control and let my tears roll down my cheeks, but, actually, it turned out quite well. I have never felt so much warmth and sympathy from them before."

Robert said he had met the skeptical "bend-over-here-it-comes-again" attitude typical for his department when a manager comes back after acquiring new skills. It didn't bother him much; it was the reaction he expected. In similar occasions before, he usually tried to explain what advantages his new skills would bring to the company. This time, he had no need for explaining; instead, he had kept his calm, responding to the gibing with a smile. The Monday morning meeting with his management team went smoothly, and, to his surprise, many of his direct reports had assumed tasks willingly instead of raising all kinds of objections, which is their usual reflex response. He has a feeling that the change had to do with his having acted differently, but he cannot point to a specific example. "Let's see if it lasts," he says. "I guess that next Monday everything will be back to usual," although he sounds far from convincing.

Jane has also had a good weekend. "I thought I'd be totally exhausted after last week, but actually I've had lots of energy," she says. "That feeling hung on when I came to work Monday, and I've gotten plenty of things done that have been hanging over me for months." Several of the others report having had similar experiences, telling the team what they have accomplished since coming back to the office.

Finally, everyone has spoken except Mark, so everybody's eyes turn to him. Reluctantly, he starts talking, saying that he has been too busy preparing a major purchase to have any time to think about anything else. The consultant, who has been mostly silent up until now, says: "You have time right now." After hesitating a moment, Mark says that he had gotten a lot to think about at the offsite, and that he had received a great deal of feedback, some of it apposite and some of it rather unfair. When asked what of the feedback he found apposite, he gives an evasive answer that is intelligible to no one around him, and he seems unable to explain what is really going on in his head, despite all the other team members trying to help him do that. The consultant, seeing that they are about to give up on Mark, says: "What's important is not what you say here; what counts is what you show in action." Jane tries to look sympathetic, but she sounds rather impatient when she asks him, "How do you feel, Mark?" He answers that, of course, it is not okay being mistrusted, as he was at the off-site, but that he is self-confident enough to bear that. Everyone can sense the wall of defensiveness he is putting up, and no one feels inclined to direct any further questions or comments to him.

Improved relations with workmates and family

The most significant effects of the team-building in this short retrospective are the changes of the members as individuals and how these have affected their social relations. The transformation might seem hard to explain—not to mention hard to believe in—considering the short time of the development process thus far. Actually, there is nothing mystical about these strong emotional effects. By opening up the emotional flow within and between team members, and removing the blinders that made it possible for them to be unaware of how they restrain themselves, the team's collective creativity, competence, and joy that have lain fallow for a long time are now free to come to life and imbue the working climate. The development program has not induced anything that was not already there as a potential of the team and its members. *The same way that mistrust causes more mistrust, a small increase in openness and trust can cause a positive dynamic that is self-reinforcing.* The streaks of euphoria expressed by team members are caused by a sense of vitality, sprung from their being able to use their full competence without having to look askance at their teammates. The strong intensity of the feelings unleashed in this particular team is mainly due to the deep level of frustration at the outset of the development process. Management teams with lesser tensions will probably have a less dramatic development process, but the outcome—drive, and a strong feeling of togetherness—will be the same.

Nor is it surprising that the changed climate in the team affected the way several of the members related to members of their families after the offsite. Working in a defensive corporate climate makes you turn off contact with your inner feelings, as well as with the feelings of other people around you, out of sheer self-preservation. Because a defensive attitude involves not being fully connected to other people, you will experience chronic frustration caused by the gap between how it is and how it could and should be: your contacts with your workmates will become shallow, and that will inevitably spill over onto your private relationships as well. In short, anytime you are using contact-avoidance as a survival strategy, that will easily become your generalized way of relating to people. Of course, the reverse is also true:

good relations with family and friends will affect the relationships among workmates in a positive way.

For this team, the impression that something mystical and incomprehensible has happened is strengthened by their difficulties in describing their experiences. When Richard, John, and the other team members try to describe what happened at the offsite, they find themselves in the same dilemma as the writer of this book: how can one depict an emotional process in a language created to describe tangible objects and events? Most people occasionally experience situations heavily charged with emotions: the magic of falling in love, or the feeling of being merged with nature when sailing or walking in the mountains. Those trying to describe such an experience to others will soon realize that it is impossible, unless the other person has had a similar experience. Accordingly, Richard's and the others' difficulties in explaining what they have experienced are due to many people before them having been part of teams getting along with more or less success—but few of them having actually experienced the profound level of openness and trust that is characterizing the top management team of Company X at this moment.

The same problem arises when the management team members try to explain their insights, when they return to work. The direct reports of the department managers could see that their bosses were behaving differently, and, of course, they were curious about what caused that change. Victor and Robert chose quite different ways to meet that curiosity. Victor gathered his co-workers and told them about his experiences, and Robert chose not to. Interestingly, both of them were able to notice positive reactions as well as positive actions that followed from their approach. In both cases, then, it is reasonable to assume that the effect was not caused by what was said, or not said, but, rather, by the different behaviors and actions they could see from their leaders. Most likely, Victor's candor and sincerity made a deeper impression on his direct reports than his verbal message, while the absence of defensiveness in Robert's response to being gibed at was also a powerful signal that something had changed.

Effects on business performance

The most interesting effect of the team-building, from a business perspective, was John's and Mary's decision to deal with an issue they have dodged before. This antic-ipates the overall purpose of the team-building process: *to generate proactive, purposeful, and result-boosting actions*. The cooperation between the marketing depart-ment and customer support has, in fact, been a recurrent item on meeting agendas of the team for years. Every time, the problem has been "solved" by Mary and John working out a plan to smooth the interactions between their departments, which was embellished by a plethora of good advice from the others. Despite that, new conflicts between representatives of their respective departments soon emerged and eventually escalated to a magnitude that made them, once again, a concern for top management. The various manifestations of cooperation between their departments made it possible, at least temporarily, for the rest of the management team to wink at the fact that it was basically the same issue being raised again and again. None of the other team members was attentive enough to realize that both John and Mary had hidden agendas, which caused both of them to withhold information and neither of them to push the measures agreed upon with enough enthusiasm for them to have any real effect. In fact, the inattentiveness of the other team members was partly driven by their receiving benefits—directly or indirectly—from enabling Mary and John to have their way each time—it diverted the focus from flaws in their own departments.

This pattern of recurrent issues not being thoroughly resolved is typical for teams operating at an insufficient level of openness and trust. The difference between a week ago and now is that the current level of trust makes covering one's back unnecessary, making it natural for everyone involved to share all relevant information, as well as to discuss the pros and cons. Should anyone, despite that, go on acting from a hidden agenda, he or she would probably be unmasked and corrected. Thus, the example of John and Mary shows how the combination of openness, trust, awareness, and a sense of overall responsibility makes it possible to solve an issue in a couple of hours that, previously, required several unsuccessful attempted measures. Accordingly, it is a good example of the core purpose of team development as presented here.

Another significant aspect of Mary and John resolving their issue is that it evidences a new culture within the team; it is not merely an example of them being given "homework" as part of the development program. Mainstream leadership programs, being more educational than developmental, usually include giving participants tasks to carry out between the offsite meetings.

The fact that this is not the case in this program has nothing to do with giving action low priority. Rather, to the contrary, Mary and John have long had the responsibility for solving their cooperation problems; their inability to do that was never an indication that they lacked understanding of how to do it. Nor did it suggest that no one else failed to tell them how to get it done. Rather, each lacked the emotional driving force necessary to help the other succeed. Similarly, the success of Company X was not a matter of heart to any of the management team members.

The overall goal of the management team development process is not to solve certain predefined operational problems. It is to build both a team culture and team standards that will compel team members to find proactive ways to improve the operation of Company X, and to insure that those improvements are carried through — regardless of whether it means crossing department boundaries or violating unwritten "this-is-how-things-are-done-here" rules. The assumption is that change of attitudes, combined with change of the interactional dynamic in the organization, will bring about progress that the piles of words, both spoken and written, have failed to generate.

Mark's behavior at the follow-up session was hardly helping him keep his position in the team. Indeed, it is too early to say whether his evasive tactics are a sign that he needs more time to digest the feedback he got at the offsite, or if his defensive attitude is too deeply rooted in his personality to be susceptible to feedback. If the latter is the case, there is quite a risk that he will mobilize people in his department in defense of their boss, isolating them from the rest of the company. In fact, the growing team spirit of awareness and overall responsibility makes it highly improbable that the other management team members would quietly allow such a wall to be built. A more probable outcome would be that Mark would be discharged from his positions as head of the purchasing department and as a member of the management team.

At this point, his defensiveness is the conclusive obstacle for him regaining Richard's and the other team members' trust, since it leaves them with no hope that he will change for the better. If they are to believe in him, Mark has to convince them that he has a realistic picture of the problems in his department, as well as a clarity about how he is contributing to them. Furthermore, he has to take firm action to solve these problems and start dealing with the attitudes and conflicts behind them. The other team members, knowing from their own experience that change is not easy, are prepared to give him time to get things straight, but they will not wait forever. Things are happening very fast in the dynamic unleashed by the deepening of the relations within the management team. Anyone clinging to outdated routines and attitudes now runs the risk of being irretrievably left behind.

The following-up process

The management team development program agreed on by Richard and the consultants was composed of three offsite occasions with at least one day of follow-up after each. The aim of the first occasion was to insure the team's processing capacity for mastering Company X's complex reality. Processing capacity is defined here as having a sufficient level of openness and trust, in combination with a profound awareness of what is important for oneself and other people, and for the success of the company. The layout and content of the second and third offsite meetings have been deliberately kept open, since they will be based on what becomes evident during the first occasion and its follow-up. The general aim for the rest of the program is to apply the team members' newly acquired competence to perform actions that generate value to the company. What actions these should be will become apparent in due time.

Three concerns will influence the teamwork at the second offsite. First, the strong feelings flaring up at the first offsite have to be addressed. Most team members disclosed much of their inner feelings, and if that is to

prove to be a good experience, they must feel acknowledged and respected for having done so in the long run. If
not, there is a considerable risk that the openness during
the offsite will be regarded as a one-time affair and the
team will bounce back to the way it functioned before,
which will leave the team members asking, "Did I say too
much?" It is crucial, therefore, that the members feel free
to express personal matters whenever they need to do so,
not only when invited to by the consultants or as part of
a scheduled activity.

The second concern, at first glance, seems to point
in the opposite direction. Development programs with
powerful elements of personal growth have a tendency to
cause participants to become introverted and self-centered,
confusing their own feelings of fulfillment with what is
beneficial for the company. Therefore, at the second offsite session, it will be important to let the development
program be enacted within the context of organizational
reality. That means the team members will turn their focus
back to matter-of-fact issues, but this time with heightened awareness of hidden agendas, defensive routines,
and habitual and counterproductive ways of thinking and
acting. This implies that they will be able to give each
other frank and unsparing feedback, which also insures a
continued high degree of personal commitment and personal growth. The seamless relation between factual and
emotional aspects of working together will make it possible to shift to personal concerns without disrupting the
main issue. The conflict between personal and operational

concerns will thereby be dissolved when a team is functioning on a deep level of openness and trust. Thus, being personal becomes the fuel for reaching an excellent result in the workaday operation.

The third concern influencing the design of the second offsite session is the unsolved problem of Mark's future in the company. It turned out that Richard, as well as the other management team members, had dodged the issue in spite of having had several opportunities to address it. His frequent follow-up meetings with Mark have focused mainly on Mark's feelings, not so much on what he is actually doing to regain trust as head of the purchasing department. Nor has anyone of the other team members made any attempts to put that issue on the agenda. In the moment of truth, it has been too sensitive to be addressed, in spite of the new spirit of openness. The reason for that might be that the other department managers' implications in the problems of the purchasing department have not been thoroughly brought to light, so an element of projection and scapegoating can be suspected in their focusing on Mark's faults. They also have little experience of using their new team processing abilities in a sharp situation, which makes them feel unsure of how to approach him. In addition, there are many exciting things going on in the aftermath of the offsite, so, quite understandably, they prefer to devote their time and energy to what gives them enthusiasm and belief in the future rather than a tiresome problem in a department that is regarded by many as not very important for the future development of the company.

Thus, the question about Mark's status in the team and in the company is still unresolved at the outset of the second offsite of the development program. The session starts with the consultants' inviting team members to share their reflections on how they have changed as leaders, and what they have accomplished due to these changes. Eventually, the limelight is directed to how Mark has dealt with the problems of his purchasing department, and how he has used the feedback he got at the first offsite. With active support from the consultants, the other team members are able to sort out their own responsibility for letting the unsatisfactory state of things go so far from Mark's responsibility as department manager. This open-hearted and self-disclosing process is a golden opportunity for Mark to let go of his defensiveness and to start scrutinizing his own behavior.

Unfortunately, he is not taking that opportunity. In fact, the emotional openness of the team seems to make him more and more uncomfortable. This, and a dawning feeling of the team members that his defensiveness is rooted in his not having enough competence to be a department manager, brings the issue of his contribution to the future development of Company X to a head. After dinner, Richard

asks Mark for a talk outside the team, and they go
to a separate room. There, Richard declares that
he has no confidence in Mark as manager of the
purchasing department, but that he will do his best
to find a more appropriate role for him in the company. Mark is shocked at first, but as the talk goes
on, he feels more and more relieved. He has felt
for a while that he has not been able to fulfill his
responsibilities as manager, and with that burden
lifted, the feelings he has suppressed well up in
him. Eventually, he and Richard return to the room
where the rest of the team is waiting, and there he
shares his reaction and reflections with all of them.
The change in his attitude makes his parting from
the offsite very emotional, with a lot of hugging
and tears. Finally, Richard drives Mark home as
they have agreed, and the other team members stay
to discuss what has happened. Some of them, especially Jane and Mary, feel guilty about Mark, so
the team spend the rest of the evening helping each
other deal with feelings evoked by his departure.

The rest of the second offsite was spent tackling several of the problems that had bothered Company X and
its top management team for a long time. Indeed, these
issues have been discussed before, but always in general
"what-should-be-done" terms. This time—and, hopefully,
from now on— management team members will hold
each other accountable for each member's contribution to

solving or not solving the problems. As one could expect, the preoccupation with Mark and the purchasing department's shortcomings obscured failings in the management of the other departments as well.

Nurtured by the new team spirit of openness and trust, and with Mark's problems put aside, a multitude of shortcomings of the other managers surface and are addressed. Affected by the general defensive culture of Company X, they have all failed to deal with inefficiency and conflicts among their subordinates, as well as among themselves; as could be expected, John and Mary were not the only ones having cooperation problems across departments. Potential synergies between the financial, the personnel, and the administrative departments had not been utilized, causing the company unnecessary expenses. Robert and his production department have been allowed to wall-in their operation for years, replacing company policies with routines of their own. As you might remember, Susan raised that issue early in the first offsite of the team development program, only to get a mix of excuses and non-binding promises.[65] Now, the whole team, Robert included, engage in finding out how Susan and her people can best support the production managers in personnel matters. This is another example of how an issue fraught with conflict goes from being unsolvable to being easily dealt with when a sufficient level of openness and trust is attained.

---

[65] See chapter 3, p. 86.

As these operational matters were successfully addressed and managed, a more forward-directed and strategic issue was brought up: looking at Company X and the departments from a perspective of change. The financial control, HR strategy, and other governing principles of the company were adapted to the protected and static situation that prevailed before Company X took the step from exclusive supplier to a player on an open market. At the present moment, however, these departments were stumbling blocks on the road to a more competitive company, rather than a force propelling the change process. The team members were also beginning to realize that their leadership style is fairly suitable for assigning tasks, but not for carrying through changes of behavior, mindset, and other cultural aspects of the company.

This points to a crucial aspect of the management team development program: the need for individual leadership development. The team members' enhanced awareness of problems and possibilities will be of no value to the company unless each of them assumes a leadership that transforms their insights into operational reality. Therefore, the second offsite of the program was concluded with team members helping each other find a very challenging task for each of them. The purpose was to help them break through the personal limitations crippling their impact as leaders. For example, John was given the task of having a talk with a "difficult" subordinate, while Jane was to rise up and give a speech in a situation with people unknown to her. Of course, by now, they all know that completing the task given to them will not be enough to maintain credibility in the team. They are also expected to deal with all the problems that have come up for discussion, as well as all the other problems not yet identified, which they will find when they return to their daily work.

Already, at the first follow-up after the second offsite, management team members were able to confirm that the once-sluggish organization of Company X was about to move. A significant sign was that the habitual grumbling over incompetence of the management, or of people in other departments, was about to be replaced by people focusing on solving the problems instead. This is probably a reaction to the department managers' new way of dealing with ingrained conflicts: addressing and solving them instead of dodging them. Most of all, however, the changed attitude among co-workers is a reflection of the new open, trustful, and optimistic "can-do" attitude they sense from their bosses.

At the same time, the first manifestations of resistance to change were detected in every department, although they were most evident in production and customer relations. The resistance came mainly from informal leaders anticipating the demolishing of their power bases, and from people who have built a comfortable existence in the permissive culture of Company X in the past. Many of the top managers had direct reports who—directly, or indirectly—fomented resistance in their sub-departments. Robert had not succeeded in convincing all of his direct reports that change was for real this time, and nothing that could be weathered by pretending it would pass. Mary met similar reactions from her co-workers, and it became clear that she had to deal with some very strong informal leaders to change the attitudes in her department.

On the basis of this resistance, it was decided that the third offsite should include, not only the top management team, but the full management teams of all departments. The purpose was to help top managers implement the new corporate culture in their departmental management teams. The discussions about change and resistance had shown that insufficient levels of openness and trust in these teams were an impediment for the intentions of top management's reaching out to all parts of the organization. By expanding the participation in the program, top management and the consultants wished to create a system of change-promoters large and powerful enough to make it possible to increase Company X's competitiveness in the shortest possible time. From that perspective, having to persuade the lower level managers in every single detail to be changed would not be good enough. Every single manager would have to be a step ahead, actively pushing things in the right direction.

The production department management team was about the size of the top management team, so they formed one group at the third offsite. The other departmental management teams were smaller, so, after a long discussion among the top managers, it was decided that managers from the marketing and customer support departments would form one group, and those from the

IT, personnel, administration, and financial departments would form another. Altogether, 30 managers were now directly involved in the development program.

As a result of their new understanding about the importance of feedback, it was natural for the department heads to participate with their own teams on the same conditions of giving and taking feedback. Richard, whose team was scattered over three different groups, joined the team of consultants, now enlarged to six. This made it possible for him to take in the whole organization, and it gave him an opportunity to practice coaching of teams and single managers under his leadership. It was also important that Richard clearly show he was in charge of the change process and that the consultants had a secondary role. If it looked like the reverse was true, Richard's credibility as leader of the company would be at risk.

Because of the expansion of the development program from nine to 30 people, two more offsite gatherings were scheduled to insure that everyone in the management system would understand the step between what ought to be done and actually doing it. The process in the three groups followed a pattern of resistance and breakthrough similar to the development in the top management team during their first offsite. The levels of openness and trust attained in these three groups were not quite as deep as they were in the top management team, mainly because the frustration was lower among B-level managers. However, since issues are usually less complex the closer to the concrete operational business they are, they do not need to reach the depth necessary for dealing with top management issues. Nevertheless, there were strong emotional moments in all three groups, and the level of openness and trust obtained was estimated to be enough for propelling the change process, that is, dealing with resistance, inciting enthusiasm, and implementing a culture of responsibility and accountability.

Back at the office after the third offsite, Richard made some organizational changes. The purchasing department was made part of the finance department, and the new purchasing manager was placed under Victor's leadership. The controller function of the finance department was reinforced, giving Victor responsibility for monitoring whether the other departments were reaching their financial goals or not. This promoted him from an administrator to a person central to the management of the company.

The biggest single change, in terms of expanded influence in the company, concerned Susan and her personnel department. Before the change process began, they mainly had an administrative function: they were assigned the role of human resources consultants to be used by the other departments. If they met no demand for their services, which usually was the case except for simple routine tasks, they could do nothing. As a result, John and Robert had preferred hiring external HR consultants who had no obligation to report to Richard and the top management team. Susan's frustration, therefore, had been of a kind that many in-house consultants can recognize. She was expected to solve problems, but she was not given the power and authority she needed to succeed. Now, Susan was given the role of "human resource controller," exercising supervision of every aspect of human behavior important to the company's success: values, attitudes, leadership styles, Richard's way of managing the company, and, most important, the level of openness and trust in management teams and other groups of strategic importance.

The transformation of Susan's role was propelled by a growing insight that the vital change dynamic and the new cooperation culture were fragile flowers that demanded careful attention. Otherwise, there was a considerable risk of the departments relapsing into their former behaviors, which, in the short-term, would slow development, and, in the long-term, would thwart faith in the future of the company. In their new role, Susan and her closest reports would be able to move freely everywhere in the company, making sure that insufficiencies in behavior and interaction were acknowledged by the manager responsible for them. Thus, like Victor, Susan became a key player in the management of Company X.

It turned out that there were two impediments for Susan and her staff shouldering their new responsibilities. First, the department was flooded with administrative tasks. That problem was easily resolved by spreading out the personnel administration, making it a responsibility for every department to handle their own daily personnel matters. Second, and not as easily dealt with, was a widespread reluctance to address conflicts among Susan's staff, making it hard for them to exercise the authority they needed in their new role. To surmount that, it was decided that the whole department should undergo a development process similar to the one the managers had gone through, to increase their courage and their status in the rest of the company. In addition to that, Susan and her closest co-workers took a comprehensive training program in coaching, focused on how to use attention, awareness, and courage to secure a sufficient level of openness and trust in teams at different levels of an organization. Step by step, they grew into their new responsibilities.

An evaluation of the change program one year later showed that the financial result and market position of Company X had improved considerably. The zeal at the beginning of the process was replaced by assiduous everyday improvements. At the same time, employee surveys showed that job satisfaction and wellbeing continued to score very high. Some frustration over the change process being too slow had surfaced a couple of months after the last offsite. Top management had gradually realized that some people holding key positions in the departments neither had the ability nor the will to be part of the renewal of the company, which called for time-consuming dismissals and recruiting steps. This also applied to the personnel department, which took almost a year to assume their new role in a way that made any difference to the rest of the company.

Even so, no traces of the dejection marking the company a year before were detected. On the contrary, there were strong feelings of hope for the future of Company X. With all these aspects taken into account, the management concluded that the change process had been a great success. They were also fully aware of the risk of letting their success become an excuse for leaning back in contentment. However, they also know they can still trust the market, continuously, to keep them on their toes.

APPENDIX.
SELECTED PSYCHOLOGICAL DEFENSE MECHANISMS

The psychological defense mechanisms described here were selected because they all belong to "normal" psychology, that is, they are commonly used in everyday life, at work as well as in social interactions. Primitive defense mechanisms associated with psychopathological states were omitted, as these are primarily relevant in the context of individual therapy, *i.e., repression*: defending oneself against an unacceptable impulse by making it inaccessible to the conscious mind; *denial*: simply denying reality despite evidence for it; and *rationalization*: giving oneself good reasons for irrational actions or reactions. The remaining mechanisms discussed here are all highly relevant for understanding team behavior: *Isolation of affect* or *Intellectualization*; *Reaction Formation*; *Displacement*; *Projection*; *Introjection*; and *Regression*.

Isolation of affect/Intellectualization

As the name implies, affect isolation means omitting from consciousness the emotional aspects of a situation, or a memory. Intellectualization reinforces affect isolation by preoccupying the mind with cognitive aspects of a situation. People using this defense mechanism can neutrally and objectively describe situations involving themselves that, by all reason, should evoke strong feelings, yet, they speak as if they are talking about someone else.

Affect isolation plays an important role when one is facing a threat or catastrophe. It helps us to keep our "cool" in situations where an emotional reaction would impair our ability to act rationally. The emotional reaction is suspended until the dangerous situation is warded off.

Some people develop affect isolation as a general defensive attitude, not only to handle crises, but to deal with their everyday life. This leads to a confined emotional life and, subsequently, to loss of life quality. That doesn't mean they always act aloof or distant; on the contrary, persons with an inclination to affect isolation are often sociable, at least as long as they can avoid emotional stress. However, when deeply affected by emotions, they tend to disconnect their inner life, which makes them inaccessible for deeper contact with other people.

Reaction formation

Reaction formation means inhibiting an impulse by doing the opposite. The classical example is how a child can deal with negative feelings they get from a younger sister or brother. The reaction of envy, rage, and a wish that the "impostor" would disappear, is countered by the child's being excessively caring and protective of a newborn sibling. Succumbing to the destructive impulse by enacting just a small part of it would inevitably arouse the parents' anger, so the reaction formation serves a twofold purpose: it controls the impulse and, at the same time, it insures the older child will continue to receive the parents' affection.

Displacement

Displacement differs from reaction formation by allowing the forbidden impulse to be enacted. However, the action is not directed toward the source triggering the impulse; instead, it is diverted toward a less threatening target. A person being unfairly rebuked by his boss might feel an inclination to reject the accusation furiously, but he does not dare to jeopardize his job by doing so. Instead, he bawls his wife out when he comes home. She might be too afraid of him to bawl back, so, instead, she scolds her son for some trifle; he, in his turn, goes angrily to his room, kicking the cat on his way.

Displacement satisfies the immediate need for reducing emotional tensions, but in a way that causes problems in interactions with others. There is great risk that the targeted person will feel unfairly attacked, and will react by withdrawing or retaliating. The system of corrective feedback—necessary for enabling people to navigate in the social world—collapses, since the one targeted by a reaction is not the person who caused the reaction. This makes it practically impossible to get to the bottom of workplace conflicts. The cause–effect chains become so intertwined and blurred that root causes cannot be separated from secondary reactions.

Projection

Our apprehension of other people is founded both on *perceptions*: the reality we invent with our senses; and *projections*: qualities we attribute to others based on our interpretations of what we perceived. These attributions are built partly on our experience, and partly on our attitudes, emotions, and psychological needs. The more emotions involved, the harder it gets to assess another person objectively.

Defined this way, projection is part of the everyday life of normal individuals. Social interaction gets its meaning from our capacity to ascribe intentions and inducements to other people. People who are unable to project in this way are severely socially handicapped, because the actions of other people would make no sense to them.

However, this ubiquitous phenomenon can also be used as a psychological defense mechanism, i.e., as a means of distorting reality to protect one's self-esteem. Imagine an interaction between two persons, A and B. They are two distinct individuals, meaning that somewhere in the A + B system there is a boundary dividing the field into one part belonging to A and the other part belonging to B. What is on A's side of that boundary is A's responsibility; what is on B's side is B's responsibility.

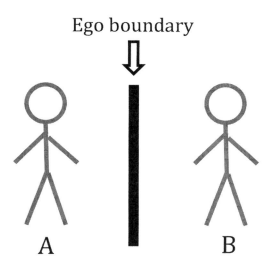

Figure 1

Using projection as a defense mechanism means one must disown some aspect of oneself—a trait, a feeling, or a behavioral pattern—and regard it as belonging to another person. Usually, the disowned aspect is something evoking guilt or shame and, therefore, is a threat to the projector's self-esteem. Instead of taking responsibility for this aspect of his or her own personality by acknowledging and processing it, the projector blames, or regards it as an aspect of, the person onto whom he has projected it.

One way of describing projection is to regard it as a blurring, or a transgression, of the ego boundaries between A and B in Figure 1. It is as if the projecting part A moves the boundary between himself and B, making the disowned parts of his own behavior appear to belong on B's side of the boundary.

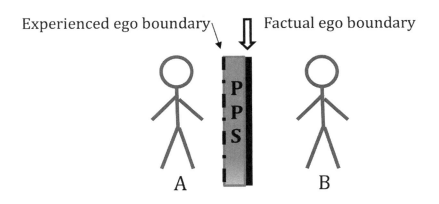

PPS = Projected Part of Self

Figure 2. Projection

The shadowed part in the figure represents qualities that belong to A but are apprehended by him as belonging to B. This ego boundary manipulation—generally carried out unconsciously—blurs the communication between A and B, because it makes it difficult to distinguish who is who in their interaction. B, being targeted by the projection, will probably regard the communication from

A as incomprehensible or unfair; while A, being under the impression that he is addressing B, is actually talking to himself.

Projections appear in many different forms. Some of them, usual in an organizational context, are:

Projection of responsibility

When we fail to fulfill our ambitions by not achieving our goals, it is tempting to blame that failure on somebody or something else outside ourselves. This can be seen at work as well as in private life: I would have been a happy and successful person had not my parents been so mean; If my spouse had been more supportive, I could have fulfilled my dreams; If it were not for my colleagues being lazy, my boss being lousy, the suppliers being sluggish, and the customers being querulous, my career would have skyrocketed. The excuses can be varied endlessly, but all of them have in common that the responsibility for how we manage our lives is projected onto the other people around, which results in our own passiveness, resignation, and embitterment.

Sometimes, it can be difficult to see through a projection. Adults are seldom totally out of contact with reality in their projections. Parents might indeed have been mean, a spouse excessively controlling, and the boss lousy. The projective quality lies in using these circumstances as an excuse for not assuming responsibility for one's own failures. Only when an individual acknowledges that responsibility, will he or she will be able to change his or her life.

Scapegoating

In times of stress and uncertainty—normalcy in many companies today—it is not unusual that some team member will be pointed to as the person impairing the work of the whole team.

When the scapegoat is appointed, all team members can project their own shortcomings and undesired traits onto him or her: incompetence, lack of responsibility, malevolence, or any other characteristic the team members want to disown.

Scapegoating is aggravated in situations marked by uncertainty, infighting, and lack of trust. To rid themselves of feelings of insecurity, team members might spotlight the most insecure teammate, often in a way that makes that person even more insecure. This pattern does not cease to exist if the scapegoat is excluded from the team. When that occurs, the former second-most insecure team member runs a considerable risk of being cast in the place of the scapegoat.

Bullying

Bullying is a more primitive form of scapegoating, mostly occurring among school-age children, but not unusual in workplaces as well. The strong wish to blend in and be accepted, combined with an immature self-esteem, gives rise to an inclination to see unwanted aspects of one's own personality as belonging to someone else. These aspects are repressed by exerting harassment or physical violence against those being identified with them. By attacking a person who is characterized as "weak," the bully attacks his own weakness.

The brutal course of bullying is often exacerbated by the use of the defense mechanism displacement (see above). The bullying situation makes it easy for the bullies to make their victims suffer for anger and frustration emanating from other situations.

Prejudice

Another phenomenon similar to scapegoating and bullying is prejudice against other social groups. It is rooted in our inclination to define ourselves by drawing a line between us and "not-us." Furthermore, the social regularization of what is to be considered normal is maintained by pointing to what is deviant. This opens for projections, *i.e.,* us blinking at our own deviations and projecting them onto "the others." The proclivity for doing this seems to increase the closer we ourselves are to the boundary between normal and deviant. Consider the following example:

> A former petty thief had been hired in a small company as part of his social rehabilitation. All employees of the company accepted him, doing whatever they could to help him break with his former life — that is, all employees but one: the janitor. His position was: "You should not get mixed up with that kind of person."

Disregarding any personal experiences that might have had impact on the janitor's attitude, it is reasonable to assume that his aversion comes from his position as the lowest ranked person of the company, who thus feels the need to stress the distance between himself and someone even lower on the social ladder. This is consistent with sociological research, which shows that prejudice is more prevalent among people from lower social classes.[66] Following the same logic, it is reasonable to assume that people who are violently opposed to homosexuality will not be counted among those who have the most solid heterosexual identity.

Introjection

Introjection, like projection, implies tampering with the ego boundaries separating person A from person B, but instead of ridding oneself of some undesired part of one's own personality by placing it outside oneself, as is the case with projection, introjection means regarding some aspect of another person as belonging to oneself, and, consequently, as something one should feel responsibility for. Thus, introjection is mirroring projection, which can be seen when comparing figure 2 above with figure 3 below.

---

[66] Carvacho, H.; Zick, A.; Haye, A.; González, R.; Manzi, J.; Kocik, C.; and Bertl, M., *On the relation between social class and prejudice: The roles of education, income, and ideological attitudes.* European Journal of Social Psychology, 45, pp. 272–285 (2013).

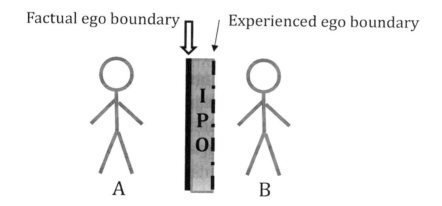

IPO = Introjected Part of the Other

Figure 3. Introjection

The shadowed part here represents qualities belonging to B but apprehended by A as belonging to himself. It can be positive aspects of other people that the introjecting person wishes to incorporate into his own personality: Small children might feel powerful in the presence of their parents, due to identification and introjection of the parent's power. Supporters of a charismatic leader introject his alluring persona, making themselves feel more energetic and less mundane. A boss boosting his own ego by taking credit for an idea that actually comes from one of his subordinates can also be described as introjecting the creativity of the other person, regarding it an aspect of his own personality.

It is more difficult to understand the reasons for introjecting negative qualities. The classic example is the beaten child idealizing the abusing parent and taking the blame himself for the maltreatment: "Mum beats me because I'm worth it." Psychologically, this is a way of maintaining the image of the good and protective parent; "I'm bad" is a far less threatening thought for a child than assuming the mighty parent to be evil. This logic can be expressed: "I'd rather be a sinner in heaven than an angel in hell."

In everyday life, introjection of guilt is ubiquitous. Most people are inclined to assume guilt for negative emotional reactions of others with whom they are interacting, regardless of whether they have caused them or not. This inclination is a main obstacle for our giving each other sincere feedback; instead, we "protect" each other from feelings of discomfort that might only exist in our imagination. This misplaced consideration blurs the interaction with other people, depriving us and those around us of information needed for navigating in the social world, and for our own growth as human beings.

Regression

Regression means returning to a previous stage of psychological development. A school-age child becoming clingy and using baby talk, or a person in his 40's coping with his aging crisis by acting like a teenager, are both examples of regression. Regressive behavior is common in situations where people experience both physical and psychological threat. Most organizational changes feel threatening, at least for some of the persons involved, and will, consequently, increase the risk of people regressing into immature behavior, such as clinging to some authority or hoping for a magical solution.

Sigmund Freud compared this psychological development to an army advancing in a foreign country. The recently conquered terrain binds part of the army, while the rest moves on. When the advancing force is met with superior resistance, it is compelled to withdraw to a position that can be defended with the use of less power. Similarly, psychological regression means retiring to a developmental stage offering comfort and safety, and requiring less psychological strain.

Regression is a component in all other psychological defense mechanisms, except *intellectualization* and *repression*.[67] Displacement, projection, and introjection are adequate elements of the psychological functioning of small children, but, with growing maturity, they should be replaced by more reality-oriented coping strategies.

Regression is not always to be considered a defense mechanism. Adults relaxing with playful sporting activities, joking, or engaging in creative pursuits, are examples of *regression in service of the ego*. As the term implies, this reviving of the childish energy and mental flexibility is strengthening the adult ego, not the opposite.

---

[67] *Repression* means expelling a thought or impulse from consciousness. For further explanation of repression, and of other defense mechanisms not discussed here, see Freud, A, *The Ego and the mechanisms of defense* (London: Hogarth Press and Institute of Psycho-Analysis, 1937); or McLeod, S. A., *Defense Mechanisms* (2009), retrieved from www.simplypsychology.org/defense-mechanisms.html